ADVANCED *INTERNET* TYCOONS' *SECRETS*

How To Create A 7-Figure Business; Selling Insights On The Web

BY:

Brian C. Guan

ALL RIGHTS RESERVED.

Before This Document Is Duplicated Or Reproduced In Any Manner, The Publisher's Consent Must Be Gained. Therefore, The Contents Within Can Neither Be Stored Electronically, Transferred, Nor Kept In A Database. Neither In Part Nor Full Can The Document Be Copied, Scanned, Faxed, Or Retained Without Approval From The Publisher Or Creator.

COPYRIGHT © BY BRIAN C. GUAN 2022.

TABLE OF CONTENT

ADVANCED INTERNET TYCOONS' SECRETS

TABLE OF CONTENT

INTRODUCTION

WHAT IS A COMPUTERIZED TYCOON?

HOW TO BECOME A COMPUTERIZED ABUNDANCE MOGUL?

TOP 7 WEB TYCOONS

CHAPTER ONE: CREATING YOUR PROPOSITION

PICKING YOUR PROPOSITION

25+ THOUGHTS FOR ONLINE ORGANIZATIONS TO BEGIN NOW

HOW WOULD YOU STARTUP AN EFFECTIVE INTERNET BUSINESS?

THE MOST EFFECTIVE METHOD TO BEGIN A WEB-BASED BUSINESS

THE CASE FOR CLARITY

REASONS YOU OUGHT TO BEGIN AN INTERNET-BASED BUSINESS

3 MOVES TOWARD MAKING AND KEEPING UP WITH CLIENT LUCIDITY

8 MOVES TOWARD BUILDING AN EFFECTIVE INTERNET-BASED COURSE BUSINESS

CHAPTER TWO: TESTING YOUR DEAL

WHY YOU SHOULD CONTINUOUSLY SELL BEFORE YOU MAKE

WHAT ISSUES COULD SEEM WHILE SETTING UP A BUSINESS ON THE WEB?

WHAT TO SELL ON THE WEB: HOW TO TRACK DOWN ITEMS TO OUTSOURCE

WHAT TO SELL ON THE INTERNET: SETTLING ON TOP-SELLING ITEMS

WHAT TO SELL ON THE WEB: WHERE TO SELL THINGS ON THE WEB

THE MOST EFFECTIVE METHOD TO SELL ON THE WEB: HOT SELLING STYLISH THOUGHTS

WEB-BASED SELLING THOUGHTS: OBTAINING ITEMS WHEN YOU'RE STUCK

INSTRUCTIONS TO SELL ITEMS ONLINE EFFECTIVELY

24 METHODS FOR MAKING YOUR MOST MEMORABLE INTERNET BUSINESS DEAL (WITHOUT SPENDING A TON)

THE FORCE OF FAME

THE STRENGTH OF WEB-BASED COMMERCIAL CENTERS IN THE RETAIL BUSINESS
4 MOTIVATIONS BEHIND WHY A WEB-BASED BUSINESS IS THE BEST SPECULATION YOU WILL AT ANY POINT MAKE

RUNDOWN

INTRODUCTION

ATTITUDE SHIFT

While it tends to be enticing to accept that the most extravagant and best citizenry have additional hours to achieve their objectives, everybody has a similar measure of time every day. How those 24 hours are made due can improve things significantly. Effective individuals accomplish objectives by developing the right propensities and taking on the right attitude toward life's battles. By replicating the methodologies utilized by the people who have previously accomplished great desires, perusers will likely grasp how moguls and even tycoons think and why their choices frequently bring enormous benefits.

The main achievement propensity moguls create is the capacity to imagine and seek after a more prominent reason throughout everyday life. For some individuals, it's barely noticeable a calling or an inborn ability to drill down bothersome, even dreaded, future results that may never happen. Envisioning undesirable outcomes is less difficult and less scary than having faith in an optimal variant of the far-off future. At the point when somebody distinguishes an extreme objective throughout everyday life, nonetheless, that goal gives guidance and motivation. That directing vision can keep a promising specialist from falling prey to a tough situation in which similar day-to-day undertakings are performed carelessly to keep up with business as usual. More important reason can likewise prompt the inventiveness and mental fortitude important to seek satisfying, enhancing work rather than staying with occupations that only cover month-to-month living expenses.

In the wake of recognizing a daily existence desire, would-be tycoons ought to look at their opinion on riches and accomplishment. Like everybody, sprouting business visionaries have two fighting characters inside: a legend and a lowlife. The legend addresses extreme potential and the commitment that everybody is completely fit for acknowledging innate gifts and qualities.

The bad guy, then again, addresses the perfect inverse; the reprobate is the epitome of narrow-mindedness and self-uncertainty and intends to undermine the legend's endeavors at every step. What character is not set in stone by which stories business visionaries accept to be valid about themselves? The people who pay attention to the form of the story in which they are powerless, uncouth, and without future commitment will favor the antagonist. Then again, the people who have faith in their capacity to develop their abilities further will be encouraged to show the capability of a legend.

Developing a mogul mentality and creating achievement propensities isn't a cycle that can happen out of the blue. To seek after objectives others accept to be unreachable, a hopeful tycoon should take time and be determined to reinforce the legend inside. Keeping a positive, legendary cordial outlook could require restricting communications with pessimistic individuals, employing individual achievement mentors, and meeting steady objectives like clockwork. Whenever sought after reliably, intrinsic potential and inside certainty will make levels of monetary flourishing, further developed well-being, professional autonomy, and individual joy that were once remembered to be incomprehensible.

What Is A Computerized Tycoon?

Beginning a web business has always been more complex. Many people are making full-time pay and working part-time hours from the solace of their own home, and on the off chance that you wish to fasten them continue to peruse. Get familiar with the principal essentials of online business and the words and terms you'll need to see to begin and become a computerized tycoon. The simple and basic because of starting a profitable web-based business all made sense bit by bit. Computerized Moguls do not just exist; they're made every day. Most have made their fortunes not by making applications, games, or new interpersonal organizations, things far off for the run-of-the-mill individual, yet by making selling and purchasing local area online as normal as baking, beginning a business, getting in shape, dating counsel, even a method for shuffling. This and the way forward for business is Currently.

Advanced business characterizes as a business that obscures the computerized and actual universes as individuals, businesses, and things interlace and criticize each other through innovation:

A computerized abundance tycoon has more than **$1 million** in computerized resources, barring their main living place and any actual merchandise.
They are additionally alluded to as web tycoons.
Computerized resources are whatever can be put away on a PC or in the cloud or have a web-based presence, as it were. Like a YouTube channel, it has yet to have an actual presence and makes many dollars for somebody. Individuals could imagine that turning into a computerized abundance tycoon is unthinkable because they need to be sufficiently educated to put resources into the right innovation. Yet, anyone could become a computerized abundance tycoon with exploration and learning.

How To Become A Computerized Abundance Mogul?
Very much like an ordinary mogul, they generally began at Nothing. Thinking about an individual who began making YouTube recordings and is making millions out of it. He, likewise, had begun with Nothing.
We will jump further into the cycle by considering an individual named "Alex" who needs to begin a YouTube channel. Here are the means you can follow to turn into a web mogul - :

Stage 1 - Have A Strong Arrangement Set up

Having a strong arrangement set up before bouncing into the universe of web entrepreneurship is significant.

It isn't just about having the right range of abilities, yet additionally the right outlook and a decent arrangement. Web requires tolerance more than you naturally suspect.

Alex necessities to construct an arrangement for what will be his channel name.

Would He Make Nondescript Recordings Or Not?
How he will shoot, alter and do Website design enhancement of his recordings. Which programming will be great for him to make his recordings seriously engaging?

How Could He Begin By Making A Video?
Individually when he responds to inquiries, he comes to a strong arrangement that responds to most inquiries and will work on the arrangement far ahead.

Stage 2 – Construct A Plan

Having a strong arrangement has neither rhyme nor reason when you don't have a plan to follow. The plan makes things more basic and more feasible.
For our situation, Alex will construct a plan for:
- *How Will He Make A Video?*
- *How Will He Advance The Video?*
- *What Will Be His Way Of Dealing With Developing The Channel?*

Alex will fabricate a cycle that he will investigate for the video and make content. From that point forward, he will shoot the video and alter it to prepare it to transfer on the web. Notwithstanding, he can likewise prearrange two recordings all at once to secure the plan and might employ somebody to alter the recordings.

All in all, you want to create a cycle that is:
- *Time-productive*
- *Cost-productive*
- *Simple To Work*

Stage 3 – Remain Fixed On Your Objectives And Keep Major Areas Of Strength For An Ethic

If you desire to succeed and accomplish your objectives, you want to foster areas of strength for an ethic and be centered around the objective.

Solid hard, working attitudes can make you what you couldn't imagine.

The main part of building a brand in the cutting-edge world is having major areas of strength for an ethic that makes serious areas of strength for individuals.

You can fabricate areas of strength for individuals by being straightforward with them. Not to advance things you don't have any desire to do.

What Can Our Personality Alex Do?

We should assume he is in the men's preparing specialty; he can suggest individuals facewashes given the idea of their skin instead of advancing an item that pays the most.

Stage 4 - Market Your Abilities Or Business

Showcasing is the method involved with conveying the worth of an item or administration to likely clients. It means a lot to showcase your abilities or business to get more clients and clients.

Promoting isn't just about publicizing. It's likewise about building connections, recounting your story, and making it simple for individuals to track you down.

The showcasing system ought to be arranged after making a present moment and long-haul objective for the organization or business.

The showcasing system ought to incorporate a portion of these means:
- *Characterizing What Your Objectives Are*

- *Distinguishing The Interest Group*
- *Make A Viable Advertising Plan*
- *Carrying out That Arrangement*

Stage 5 - Be Available To New Open doors and Continue To Master New Abilities

There are no more 90s where you can find a new line of work and need to stress over losing it early. These days if you are not creating anything useful for an organization, you are only one email away from your end.

In the period of computer-based intelligence and mechanization, many individuals are concerned that they will lose their positions. Nonetheless, it is a fact that only some positions will get supplanted by innovation.

The new positions are more imaginative and require a greater number of abilities than previously. Individuals ought to be available to new open doors and continue to acquire new abilities to remain on the ball.

For Alex, learning Website Design Enhancement for YouTube is vital, which changes step by step. What worked a couple of years prior may not work presently.

Coming up next are a portion of the available ranges of abilities that Alex ought to have:
- *Web-based Entertainment Showcasing*
- *Website Improvement (Web Optimization)*
- *Email Showcasing*
- *Paid Publicizing (Google Adwords)*

How Computerized Abundant Moguls Spend Their Riches

It's not been stowed away from anybody how troublesome it is to spend computerized crypto abundance in reality. Indeed, there are a few things for which computerized tycoons sprinkle out their money.

As per a new CNBC study, nearly half of millennial moguls hold 25% or more of their abundance in cryptographic money.

Computerized Abundance Tycoons

They likewise observe a few fundamental guidelines to keep up with their portfolio risk instead of simply putting some into cryptographic forms of money. Lately, organizations are joyfully tolerating bitcoin as a method for paying for wares. Because of this, crypto tycoons are sprinkling their abundance into purchasing things in reality.

1. *Yachts*

In the principal quarter of this current year, Swiss yacht organization "Sea Freedom" declared that they would acknowledge crypto as an installment door.

Peter Hürzeler, overseeing accomplice of Sea Autonomy, additionally referenced, "Digital currencies have turned into a basic piece of the present world and will turn out to be progressively significant."

2. *Land*

The land has been from the get-go tolerating digital currencies for extravagant properties. But home is one of the rising organizations that allows you to list properties for cryptographic money.

3. *Vehicles*

Purchasing luxurious vehicles should be possible through crypto too. With high total assets, people are becoming involved with sports vehicles.

Yet, vehicles have been at the center of attention to trade vehicles employing cryptographic money and working beginning around 2016.

4. *Tungsten*

Also, tungsten in the times when crypto moguls are fixated on it.

Indeed, even some computerized abundance tycoons are getting 3D shapes of this interesting and incredibly weighty component as an image of progress.

It was truly newsworthy when a gathering of mysterious crypto holders purchased a 3D shape weighing 900 kg alongside an NFT for $250K in Ethereum.

5. Craftsmanships

With the rise of NFT, fine arts have been at the center of attention for a couple of months.

Individuals make NFTs of fine arts and sell them on various stages like Opensea, Supercar, and Rarible.

TOP 7 WEB TYCOONS

It's no big surprise how the web has developed and delivered many moguls in an extremely limited capacity to focus.

Here are the Main seven web moguls - :

1. Jeff Bezos (Organizer Behind Amazon)

Jeff made a significant part of his abundance from his organization Amazon which he began in 1994.

His total assets as of now remain at $146 Billion.

2. Bill Gates (Pioneer Behind Microsoft)

Bill Gates began his product-based web organization "Microsoft" Wayback in 1975 with his companion Paul Allen..

His total assets right now remain at $123.6 Billion.

3. Larry Page (Pioneer Behind Google)

Larry Page established Google in September 1998 with companion Stanford Ph.D. Student, Sergey Brin.

His total assets presently remain at $95.9 Billion.

4. Larry Ellison (Organizer Behind Oracle)

Larry Ellison established Oracle, one of the underlying programming-based organizations, in 1977 in California, US.
His total assets presently remain at $93.1 Billion

5. Sergey Brin (Fellow Benefactor Of Google)
Sergey Brin is one of the underlying fellow benefactors of Google. He helped establish it with Larry Page in 1998 when they were both at Stanford College while seeking postgraduate educations in Software engineering.
His total assets as of now remain at $92.3 Billion.

6. Steve Ballmer (Previous Chief Of Microsoft)
Steve joined Microsoft as a worker in 1980, turned the organization's President in 2000, and remained firm on his footing until 2015.
His total assets at present stand at $84.2 Billion.

7. Mark Zuckerberg (Pioneer and Chief Of Facebook)
Mark Zuckerberg is one of the underlying individuals to get into building an informal community where individuals can interface. He established Facebook in the year 2004 at 19 years old.
In any case, Facebook has stayed under security worries for a couple of years.
His total assets at present stand at $63.1 Billion.

With the ascent of cryptographic forms of money and NFTs, computerized abundance tycoon is a typical term to pay attention to. It accompanies much chance as Bitcoin is 45% down in half a year.

A ton of moguls who just discuss about crypto troublemakers currently become quiet for a couple of months.
Rest depends on you and how much risk you can endure.

Will Non-Specialists Become Computerized Moguls?
Totally YES. With the way that given sufficient opportunity, difficult work, and brilliant monetary direction, anybody can turn into a computerized

tycoon. In no way, shape or form does this imply that everybody will ultimately turn into a computerized mogul.

Like each professional decision or, in any event, evolving vocation, if commitment, center, and difficult work are not engaged with the forward cycle, we definitely will fizzle.

The Computerized world can cause you to acquire serenity to carry on with the way of life you need.

Going Forward Are A Few Abilities That Can Boost Your Income Stream Even As A Tycoon Or Newbie Online. Bon Voyage!

CHAPTER ONE: CREATING YOUR PROPOSITION

PICKING YOUR PROPOSITION

Having an extraordinary item or administration is imperatively significant for the present business people. However, many erroneously feel that their creation alone will produce mass consumerism. It will not.

You want to know how to self-make a few floods of client traffic in the progressively computerized world. To get customers, you should comprehend what their identity is and what organizations they now follow. Gain from those organizations, and expect to become approaches with them at last. Before long, you won't just be offering the web traffic to them, yet you'll claim your own.

You got to figure out how to orchestrate your web-based channels, catch and convert likely clients, and market on unambiguous social stages. Regardless of your item or administration, the objective is consistent web-based traffic.

1. **Figuring Out Internet Showcasing**

One of the most concerning issues with our school system is the need for more business venture preparation. Furthermore, one of the main pressing concerns with business people today is their off-track conviction that an extraordinary item will produce incredible clients. Getting clients to your business is craftsmanship.

The initial step to dominating this craftsmanship is understanding that your business is about your clients, not you or your item. Recognize who your fantasy clients would be and become fixated on them. Attempt to comprehend what they need and need worse than they figure out themselves.

Individuals buy an item for one of three reasons: well-being, riches, and connections. When you recognize which of those three reasons your item fits, next, you need to distinguish which bearing your client is going - away from torment or towards delight.

Clients might have comparable objectives yet various explanations behind having them.

The better you comprehend their thinking, the more you can address their issues and sell them your item.

You need to respond to the following inquiry: "where are these clients congregating?" The web upset publicizing since it permitted similar individuals to meet and talk online in one spot about their common advantages at last. Previously, you could catch pockets of these gatherings, in actuality. With the web, you can quickly arrive at your fantasy clients without anything to do or cash.

You want to recognize where your fantasy clients are congregating by understanding the top sites they visit, digital recordings they stand by listening to, YouTube recordings they watch - basically what they like. Finding them will be troublesome if you think you must comprehend your clients.

One incredible procedure for interfacing with your fantasy clients is making a Fantasy 100 rundown of organizations that, as of now, contact them. Contact these substances continually - make them know what your identity is and what your item is; ideally, they'll like it and assist with publicizing it.

1. **Developing A Promotion**

Most promotions today use a Snare, Story, and Proposition system to hinder clients from their ordinary exercises and fabricate a relationship with them by recounting a story and offering the item. The Snare, Story, and Deal is the starting point for selling anything on the web.

The snare should catch clients' eye, and you should put these where your fantasy clients gather. There's nothing that snares can't be, as they make clients stop what they're doing, even briefly.

Inside that second, you need to recount to them a story. Your 3 should increment the worth of anything you're offering and fabricate an association with purchasers. Regardless of whether they purchase anything from you, presently, they know what your identity is.

At long last, the deal is essential for them to make a move. Buying your item would be the best result;

however, even something as basic as enjoying a post or following a divert would be significant in advancing and, in the end selling your image/item.

Your Fantasy 100

When you contact your Fantasy 100, ensure you are fully informed regarding what they are doing and delivering. Additionally, get one of their items to see their interaction and what is working (and not working) for them. Make a relationship, yet in addition gain from them. Whenever you've made a relationship, help them before requesting anything. You can likewise send items to them free of charge to get criticism. If they like what they get, this would be an ideal opportunity to inquire whether they would advance your items.

It's a composition consolidating true sympathy, key association, and initiative abilities for more compelling correspondence. Correspondence is the outward sign of our viewpoints and aims. Utilized really, it can assist us with building trust in our connections and decidedly impact people around us.

Each correspondence methodology gathers impact once it associates with individuals at their center. All in all, attention to what the other individual needs. Whether we manage a youngster or many representatives, this is a generally accepted fact.

Impact expects us to place ourselves in the spot of others. It involves knowing what they genuinely need and offering it to them. This is particularly evident in undertakings.

A great many people, generally speaking, neglect to contemplate others. Alternately, the person who decides to focus on the interests of others is separate. We recollect such individuals and trust them all the more profoundly.

This doesn't mean we ought to supplant our inclinations with those of others. It implies integrating others' inclinations into our own to make significant associations with them, not only for building a group of people.
.

25+ THOUGHTS FOR ONLINE ORGANIZATIONS TO BEGIN NOW

Maintaining an independent venture certainly has its allure; however, it accompanies its arrangement of difficulties. Truly, beginning a business of any sort is difficult to work, and the initial step is coming up with something. In this guide, you are provided with many web-based business thoughts and guide you on the most proficient method to begin a private venture on the web.

Innumerable individuals have proactively taken the jump into business. Also, with the right internet-based business thoughts and a lot of sweat value, you can.

This isn't around one basic extraordinary stunt. Beginning an internet-based business works differently. To assist you with finding beneficial web-based business thoughts, we've assembled an assortment of straightforward ways of beginning a business without stopping your normal employment.

1. Numerous web-based organizations can be begun with minimal startup capital.
2. The most lucrative web-based organizations incorporate corporate guidance counseling and programming advancement.
3. Construct a web-based business in a subject or industry you are energetic and educated about.
4. This segment is for hopeful business people seeking motivation to begin a web-based business.

Claiming and keeping a web-based business allows business visionaries to bring in cash from any place on the planet. The thought is alluring and more conceivable than at any other time; however, numerous business people don't know where to begin. The main move toward beginning a productive web-based business is to find a business thought that matches your abilities and assets. Look at the best Mastercard handling suppliers to find an accomplice to assist you with tolerating installments on the web.

Whether you need to turn into a full-time business person or begin a part-time business for automated revenue, your item or administration ought to satisfy a particular shopper's need. We've gathered a progression of beneficial need-based organizations with negligible startup costs that you can begin quickly.

1. Turn Into A Web Optimization Advisor

If you know the intricate details of web search tools and have specialized abilities in stages like Google Promotions and Google Examination, turning into a Web optimization expert could be a worthwhile choice. Numerous entrepreneurs need to understand the amount an effective site design improvement (Search engine optimization) can have on their business. Begin your web-based counseling business by instructing those entrepreneurs on the force of Web optimization to assist with changing their sites and increment their transformation rates.

You could utilize your advertising abilities to the big-time proprietors the advantages of utilizing investigation information, key catchphrases, and content construction to acquire natural web traffic. If you are new to Web optimization or need to hopefully look out for any way to improve your advanced promoting abilities, there are a lot of courses out there that can assist with that.

Recollect that Google's calculations are continuously changing, so you should continue your schooling on Search engine optimization to remain pertinent and fruitful in this field.

Key Action Item: *Teach independent companies about the significance of Website design enhancement and assist them with developing their web-based presence.*

2. Turn Into An Independent Venture Expert

Assuming you have extraordinary business experience and information, why not make a business that assists hopeful business people with succeeding? As a business specialist, you could utilize your abilities to assist new entrepreneurs with starting very well and assist experienced business visionaries with staying aware of their interests. Your odds of coming out on top are more prominent if you center your procedure around a specialty part of business counseling.

It is useful to be available in the advanced business local area to add to your validity, exhibit your aptitude, and get clients.

Key Action Item: *Utilize your business experience and information to assist hopeful business people with making progress.*

3. **Turn Into An Online Entertainment Expert/Director**

Bigger ventures can enlist an office or full-time staff part to run their web-based entertainment accounts; however, private companies frequently need to deal with their virtual entertainment advertising. With such countless obligations, entrepreneurs need to be more occupied, overpowered, or uneducated about the significance of a web-based entertainment presence to invest energy in creating and executing an incredible online amusement methodology. As an online entertainment specialist, you can assist independent ventures with deciding the best methods and posting schedules and content for their major interest group. As their supporter count develops, so will your business.

Facebook and Twitter are the top business organizations, yet organizations frequently battle with additional visual stages like Instagram, Pinterest, Tumblr, and Snapchat. These stages have tremendous purchaser crowds, yet numerous organizations need to understand how large they are, how successful they can be, and how to make them work for their image. On the off chance that you have experience with web-based entertainment promoting and energy for photography, zeroing in on your advisory business on one specific stage, such as Instagram, can be an incredible method for bringing in cash while assisting different organizations with working on their substance and accomplishing their business objectives.

Overseeing and developing web-based entertainment accounts is expertise. If you have the slashes, think about becoming a virtual entertainment chief or brand expert.

You'd be liable for keeping an organization's social presence internet, fostering its social showcasing technique, overseeing efforts, and other related undertakings. It's a strong web-based business thought with a lot of interest, with occupations in online entertainment expected to develop by 10% through 2030, and it only takes a little startup money to start.

To begin, make a site, your web-based entertainment channels (develop them and use them as friendly verification to win clients!), and an installment handling framework. As you acquire insight, you can begin taking special care of a more extensive cluster of online entertainment needs, similar to profile development, effort, or brand sponsorship of the executives.

Why Start A Web-based Entertainment Executive Business?
1. The assistance-based business has few obstructions to the passage, and it's somewhat simple to begin.
2. You're ready to work for yourself and choose your procuring potential. The more experience and results you can show, the higher your administration charges can be.
3. You can transform something you're doing consistently into a lucrative movement as a web-based entertainment chief.

Key Action Item: *Assist organizations with grasping the significance of online entertainment and developing their social finishing aptitude.*

4. Turn Into A Specialty Market Online Business Retailer

There's a crowd of people for everything, regardless of whether it's just about as unambiguous as dollhouse furniture or natural canine food. You can arrive at clients looking for your items with a specialty internet business webpage. Building a business in a specialty market can assist you with separating yourself from different brands and fabricating your validity and skill. Focus on web-based entertainment, or your buyer needs to foster an item to sell on your web-based store.

To prepare your internet business, you need a web-facilitating administration with an incorporated shopping basket component or internet business programming. To improve the delivery cycle, you can work with merchants to send items to clients for your sake.

This can reduce the amount of stock you want to keep closely. You may be on to your next fruitful web-based business thought if you perceive an open door in a specific specialty.

Specialty items take care of an interesting crowd. When they get along nicely, they serve a particular local area.

Specialties could be founded on industry, segment, cost, topography, values, and item credits; from there, the sky is the limit. Truly, a specialty could be anything sufficiently explicit to focus on a little gathering of expected clients. For instance:

1. Cognizant Shoppers: think veggie-lover, maintainable, and eco-accommodating items and brands.
2. Pet People: you might penetrate somewhere near the pet kind.
3. Telecommuters: these experts have explicit properties unique to the conventional office specialist.

Why Foster A Specialty Item?
1. Specialty items are novel and, in this manner, buzzworthy. Early achievement can be all you want to drive press inclusion with zero spending plan.
2. However, niching down may be startling to some; picking a particular objective client makes it simpler to make showcasing and informing that resounds. As opposed to attempting to address a

wide, different gathering, you're conversing with a gathering of people with bunches of shared qualities.

Key Action Item: *If you have a specialty item or administration to sell, consider beginning a web-based store.*

5. Turn Into A Website specialist Or Web Designer

Suppose you are an imaginative, computerized proficient who blossoms with framing the format, visual subject, text style set and variety range of a site. In that case, independent website architecture might be a decent way for you. Assuming you have zero involvement with this field,

you can get familiar with the rudiments of website architecture and expert the apparatuses you'll require for progress, similar to Adobe XD, Chrome DevTools and word processor programming. Independent web improvement may be your sweet spot if you are keener on the coding side of building sites. If you know HTML, CSS or JavaScript and have a decent eye for tackling issues with effective fixes, you can send off help to construct alluring, simple-to-involve sites for independent companies. If you want to gain proficiency with the essentials of web improvement before sending off your full-stack vocation, you can take a basic fledgling course to get everything rolling.

Set out to utilize your specialized and innovative abilities for entrepreneurs who need to take their web-based presence to a higher level. Construct a complete portfolio, and afterwards, make your site to show off and draw in a constant flow of clients.

Key Action Item: *Turning into a website specialist or designer is an extraordinary choice for those with specialized skills.*

6. Begin A Blog Or Become A Blogger

Writing for a blog might appear to be an obsolete business system since almost everyone has one. Yet, the opposition shouldn't deflect you from beginning this internet-based business venture. If you love composing or have significant data to share, publishing content to a blog might be a productive business for you.

Beginning a blog as a business is straightforward with web designers like Weebly and WordPress; however, consistency and quality are vital to progress. To acquire a consistent following, you should ceaselessly compose and create an excellent substance that offers some incentive to your perusers. Content that directs, enlightens, or engages your perusers and encourages them to follow you.

Whenever you've dominated making steady happy, you can bring in cash through your blog by selling items like web-based courses, computerized training, digital books or online classes. You can also sell advertising area or sponsored posts.

This business technique might require investment and work to adapt, yet it tends to be productive. Note that Assuming you decide to sell computerized items, guarantee your site is dependably fine with the appropriate SSL encryption.
Contributing to a blog has progressed significantly since its origin. What was once a virtual diary has now transformed into a promoting and, surprisingly, an adaptation instrument.

Whether you bring in cash from distributing supported posts, facilitating third-get-together promotions, or selling your items, a blog is an extraordinary web-based business you can begin at home.

Beginning an effective blog is to concentrate on building a drew-in, faithful crowd. When you begin with a handful of customer-driven approach, you'll create a local space that confides in you. Also, when you can obtain trust, you can start to drive cash-flow.

That is how Mr. Cash Mustache began his well-known individual accounting blog. What started as a development has transformed into an effective business that has procured public media inclusion.

Why Start A Blog?
1. Web journals have limitless development potential. You can venture into member showcasing, online business, courses, and other web-based undertakings. Some online journals even employ a purchase membership plan to drive cashflow.
2. A blog is a mapped-out play. While you won't see those results, they will probably be more manageable for the time being. A blog stays on the web continually — or, if nothing happens until you delete it.
3. It allows you to rehearse your composition — a fundamental expertise in business and correspondence. Use apparatuses like Grammarly or Hemmingway to work on your composition.

Key Action Item: *If you are a scribe with reliable substance, you might have the option to transform your blog into a business.*

7. **Become A Menial Aide (VA)**

Do you have flawless hierarchical abilities and undertaking the board capacities? Perhaps now is the right time to effectively utilize those abilities by becoming a menial aide. VA benefits ordinarily comprise essential regulatory undertakings like entering information, making travel courses of action and noting calls. Past involvement with this field is ideal yet not needed. Platforms like TaskRabbit and Zirtual simplify the process for VA gurus to secure grounds. They allow you to create a virtual profile, pursue objectives you need to finish -for example, information research, virtual assistance or essential tasks - and start building clients.

Is it true that you are coordinated and love working in the background?

If this is true, you may be the ideal candidate to begin a menial helper (VA) business.

A VA helps business people, organizations, and leaders create their own proficient lives. There's a wide range of duties, going from organizational planning to fundamental showcasing the board and in between. Moreover, everything is done on the internet.

Why Become A VA?
1. Work with your viable customers. Regardless of whether you know toward the beginning, over the long run, you'll figure out who you love working with and how you love to help them. You can develop your business to take care of those inclinations.
2. Interface with individuals from everywhere in the world. All you want is a web association with takes care of your responsibilities, and you can get the opportunity to work with worldwide clients and experts.
3. Build your business into a workforce of VAs. Assuming you become excessively occupied or have development objectives, you can recruit and prepare VAs to work under you and increment benefits.

Key Action Item: *Become a menial aide to help others with their regulatory undertakings remotely.*

8. **Turn Into An Associate Advertiser**

If you love leaving client surveys on locales like Amazon, you might need to investigate partner promoting as a type of revenue. Informal exchange publicizing is, as yet, a colossal lead generator for some organizations. Numerous organizations will impart a part of their benefits to powerful people who will elevate their items to general society.

Partner programs separate into various degrees of contribution: unattached, related and involved. Unattached subsidiary showcasing is an essential compensation for every snap crusade that expects practically no contribution with the item you are advancing. Related partner showcasing expects you to have a little power and content on the item you are promoting, yet you need to utilize the item. Involved member showcasing may be the best, as you'll showcase an item you really use and appreciate.

If you have an individual site or web-based entertainment presence with an enormous following, partner projects might be a productive methodology for you. PR reps generally search out brand backers and powerhouses so they can send free examples.

Offshoot showcasing is when you suggest an item or administration by sharing it on a blog or virtual entertainment to your email list, on your site, or different channels. You procure a commission each time somebody changes over through your remarkable outside reference or code.

Find an associate program that suits your inclinations, individual brand, and interest group. Partner Future, ShareASale, and FlexOffers are a couple of models. Amazon has its subsidiary program, and you can look at the Shopify Partner Program.

Whenever you've joined, begin sharing. Make online entertainment posts, blog articles, messages, and other substance about how extraordinary the item or administration you're advancing are. Don't oversaturate your crowd with advertisements; in any case, you risk seeming malicious or inauthentic.

For What Reason Should You Do Subsidiary Advertising?
1. It's simple: you probably advance the items and administrations you use as of now. Presently you can get compensated for it!
2. Member promoting is an incredible wellspring of recurring, automated revenue. With the Shopify Partner Program, subsidiaries procure a normal of $58 for every client who pursues a paid arrangement and $2,000 for every In addition to reference.

Key Action Item: *Those with an enormous web-based entertainment following or online presence can channel that power into making income through offshoot promoting.*

9. Distant Technical Support

Numerous private companies need more space in that frame of mind to enlist a full-time IT representative, so when their frameworks act up, they call a PC sharp companion or relative for the most part. If you are educated and have experience dealing with PCs and organizations, you can take out their need to ask for help by offering prompt, specialized help. Although a few organizations might favor having a specialized degree, many will shift focus to your experience and information, all things being equal. You can fabricate your distant technical support business by reaching companions, family, and neighborhood entrepreneurs about their technical support needs. You can also find self-empowered technical assistance gigs on workplaces like Upwork.

Key Action Item: *Utilize your tech wizardry to offer far-off technical support.*

10. Turn Into A High-quality Art Vendor

As dealers change their deals to web-based businesses, online commercial centers for hand-tailored merchandise, such as Etsy and ArtFire, make it incredibly simple for artisans who can deliver a consistent stockpile of value high-quality items, like knitted covers or remarkable painted dish sets. On the off chance that you have a remarkable art, selling your items on an internet business webpage is an effective method for procuring pay while you're at home, making every moment count.

Startup costs for this business are very low if you buy your imaginative materials in mass from a specialty provider. If you can make and sell your fine art rapidly on a web-based store, you'll create a gain in the blink of an eye. Nearby artisans make higher progress when they advance their organizations via web-based entertainment.

If you're especially cunning, selling high-quality items would be an incredible internet-based business thought for you. Whether you make gems, photo placements, or furniture, one method for adapting your special abilities is selling items on the web. Handcrafted products are an extraordinary industry for creatives and, surprisingly, a reachable business thought for youngsters.

While you can utilize stages like Craigslist or Etsy, your online store will give you more control and simplify following and satisfying orders.

Why Sell Handcrafted Merchandise?
1. Dedicate so a lot or as brief a period as you need. It's your decision on how large you need to develop.
2. Make it on your timetable. Make your hand-tailored products on a set timetable when you have spare time or at whatever point you need.
3. Transform your enthusiasm into pay. In the same way as other web-based business thoughts on this rundown, a pioneering try supported by energy prompts a seriously satisfying encounter.

Key Action Item: *Utilize your imaginative virtuoso to sell hand-tailored creations on the web.*

11. Turn Into An Application Or Potential Site Engineer

Portable applications are more well-known than at any time in recent memory, with individuals able to pay great cash to deal with their lives from their cell phones. If you have an incredible novel thought for an application and expertise in code, you can go for it and make your application. You can also become an app developer for organizations that need to make specific applications.

The two choices expect you to know the fundamental components of a programming plan and some normal programming dialects, like SQL, JavaScript, PHP, Python, Ruby on Rails or iOS.

If you have an application thought yet need the foggiest idea about the intricate details of coding, many programming engineers hope to team up with individuals on application creation. Contingent upon your circumstance and expertise, you might have the option to make a worthwhile business out of application improvement.

If you're educated, obtain a few coding abilities and begin building. Whether it's portable applications, Shopify applications, or sites, you can make computerized items for buying or as a specialist co-op.

For instance, you can make a custom Shopify subject layout and offer it to shippers searching for a reasonable Do-It-Yourself way to plan their site. Or on the other hand, work with clients straightforwardly to construct sites and applications customized to their particular requirements.

Why Create Applications And Sites?
1. Innovation is staying put, and the interest in the specialized abilities important to construct applications and sites will keep developing.
2. There's an unending number of stages and frameworks out there. On the off chance, you get exhausted of one, learn and progress to another.

Key Action Item: *Make the following best versatile application by turning into an application designer.*

12. **Turn Into A Web Index Engineer**

Google and Bing are omnipresent; however, they will only be guaranteed to address some of the clients' necessities. If you're a specialist in a specific field, construct your web crawler that assists individuals with less information in finding what they're searching for. Your odds of coming out on top may be higher if your web crawler permits clients to embed boundaries, for example, subtopics and source type, instead of simply directing a general pursuit.

Key Action Item: Construct a specialty web index to address clients' needs.

13. **Turn Into A Dropshipper Or Begin An Independent Outsourcing Company**

If you have any desire to run an internet business webpage, you may be stressed over putting away stock. Utilizing outsourcing, you can take customer orders on an Internet store and send them outrightly to an outsider retailer for satisfaction. However long your plan of action includes selling things at a cost higher than whatever you'll pay to the outsider retailer will set your outsourcing business progress.

Do you want a distribution center loaded with stock to maintain your business? Reconsider! Outsourcing is an extraordinary method for beginning a business on a careful spending plan. You can raise a ruckus around town by obtaining a previous item from a provider and having them deal with things like bundling and satisfaction. This cycle allows you to skirt many deterrents holding up traffic going into business. All the more critically, it takes out the gamble of figuring out there's no market for your item after submitting a colossal request with a producer or provider.

Why Pick Outsourcing?
1. You don't need to stock items in a particular area, implying that your cashflow will not get tied-up in stock. There's less forthright money risk.
2. Whenever a buy is made, you submit a request with an outsider, and they handle the remainder of the interaction for you. Since you don't need to manage things like following stock or mailing bundles, outsourcing takes out a ton of expected migraines for sprouting business people.
3. No stockroom implies you can maintain your business from any place. Whether it's your family room or the cafe down the road, you choose where you need to work from.

Key Action Item: You can utilize outsourcing to host a third-get-together retailer to satisfy your web-based business orders.

14. **Start A Mentoring Business Or Show A Web-based Course:**

Because someone is having lessons in a subject doesn't imply they produced the material well. If you're perfect at making sense of things for someone in a one-on-one setting and have a greater suitable experience and information in a subject, ponders on starting an internet coaching business in that field. You can utilize video talk devices, for example, Skype, to direct coaching meetings from a distance and proposition your insight to anyone, whenever, anyplace. Consider consolidating a spending plan for promotions on Craigslist and Fiverr into your action plan.

Showing a web-based course is a low-venture online business thought for creating recurring, automated revenue. Everything you want to do is assemble a video walkthrough, make sense of a subject you know about, and afterwards, have it on your site. Although it requires exertion front and center, if you figure out how to plan a famous, high-esteem video instructional exercise series, you will bring in cash on a continuous premise as individuals keep on signing up for your course.

To begin making your most memorable internet-based course, conceptualize a theme that you know all around ok to show somebody how to do without any preparation. There's nothing that this can't be in a real sense — music creation, online entertainment showcasing, web improvement, etc.

Then, you'll need to get a screencasting application like ScreenFlow to record your screen and voice while you walk your understudies through your instructional exercise. ScreenFlow likewise accompanies an underlying video-altering suite, allowing you to shoot and cut your recordings generally on a similar stage.

Why Show A Web-based Course?
- ➢ With a web-based course, you can, in a real sense, set it and fail to remember it. Require a couple of days or weeks, contingent upon the

intricacy you're going for the gold, an internet-based course, and you could receive the rewards for quite a long time.

- ➤ You, as of now, has the information; you must share it. Centre around instructing something that you're now a specialist at, and the rest will easily fall into place, whether it's structuring iOS applications, making month-to-month financial plans, or running Facebook promotion crusades.
- ➤ Showing somebody another ability is its award. While there's certainly cash to be made showing on the web courses, helping others is dependably a fantastic involvement.

Key Action Item: *Set out to utilize your high-level information in a particular subject by mentoring understudies.*

15. Make Computerized Courses

Like mentoring, individuals worldwide could profit from you imparting your mastery to them. Beginning a web-based business that offers computerized courses to anyone interested in the point can undoubtedly bring in your cash – you can sell arranged composed materials or other downloadable substances for a charge.

Key Action Item: *Make and sell computerized seminars on a recognizable subject.*

16. Begin A YouTube Channel Or Become A Video Content Maker

YouTube makes beginning an internet-based training business particularly simple. Transfer recordings of yourself instructing watchers regarding any matter, whether fledgling or progressed, and utilize web-based entertainment to get the news out about your channel. As your number of viewers develops, you'll have the choice to adapt your recordings and create a profit from them.

Key Action Item: *Utilize your video-making skills to bring in cash through visual media on YouTube.*

17. Begin Telecoaching Or Begin A Web-based Training Business

Certain individuals searching for one-on-one assistance could need more than illustrations. Individuals who need assistance propelling their professions, working on their sustenance or seeing additional importance in their lives could profit from your training through video talk programming like Zoom or Skype. Instead of giving activities and grades, as a tell coach, you want to offer exhortation, rules and backing for your clients.

If you maintain a blog for your business or routinely post to LinkedIn about the subjects you're training, you'll show up more dependable and educated.

Have instructing abilities? Join the web-based training industry and begin instructing clients in your specialty. How? Begin by clarifying what you offer, and the outcomes clients can anticipate from your instructing endeavors.

Online mentors like Simone Seol use Instagram to get to clients that need the outcomes her training offers. On the off chance that you will go to the instructing course, web-based entertainment showcasing is an unquestionable necessity. Finding an opportunity to get guaranteed in your specific subject matter can assist with laying out you as a specialist in your field and increment validity.

Why Start An Internet Instructing Business?
1. Internet training has big-time salary potential assuming that you have strong relational abilities and can get clients results
2. There's no gatekeeping to the business. You can begin training in any subject you're learned enough to charge for.
3. Verbal promoting can be a strong client-age source once you get everything rolling.

4. Key Action Item:: Offer virtual one-on-one instruction through video talk programming.

18. <u>Make A Webcast Organization Or Send Off A Digital Recording</u>

Beyond quite a while have seen a blast in webcast accessibility and listenership, and you can profit from that by beginning your web recording organization. You can crowd the organization with any virtual broadcasts you record, yet assuming you give others – whether friends or outsiders from the internet – valuable chances to contribute their digital recordings,

your organization will probably develop rapidly. You can build the cost per web recording download as your organization develops.

If you like your voice, consider recording it for a webcast. Digital recordings are an incredible self-start venture with different adaptation choices, like beginning a blog.

This is the very thing you want to begin your web recording:
1. A Great Receiver
2. Sound Recording Programming
3. Call Recording Programming

To advance your webcast, consider teaming up with unmistakable figures as visitors to your show. Urge audience members to leave audits and share your web recording with their loved ones.

Why Start A Webcast?
1. Webcasts keep on filling in ubiquity. As per Digital broadcast Bits of knowledge, 51% of Americans have paid attention to a web recording.
2. A fruitful webcast can prompt vast potential outcomes: transform your episodes into a blog, request patrons and publicists, and make associations you would never have had the option to.

Key Action Item: *Construct a webcast following by examining something you are energetic about and learned about.*

19. Turn Into A Specialized Essayist, Publicist Or Figure Out How To Distribute Your Book

The web is loaded with marketing specialists for enlisting. Notwithstanding, few marketing experts have the specialized foundation to adequately create a instructional manual for a robust machine or appropriately convey pragmatic results. If you have experience with science and can expound on it, begin a web-based business through which individuals can enlist your specialized

composing administrations. Advertise yourself on LinkedIn, Fiverr and different platforms to attract customers.

Lett it be known: you've pondered distributing your book someday is alright. While seeing your name on a rundown of smash hits could appear to be an unrealistic fantasy, it's not excessively far unattainable.

It doesn't make any difference if it's a sci-fi novel, a promoting guide, or a kids' image book; there are many choices for effectively independently publishing your work. These incorporate publishing your composition as a virtual book with the High-level Downloads application or employing on-request printing facilities like Snippet and CreateSpace.

To sell digital books through your web-based store, introduce the Computerized Downloads application, and you'll, in a split second, have the option to computerized stock records as items. Once bought, your digital books will be shipped off to your clients through email or as a direct download connection.

If you decide to sell actual duplicates of your book, you'll have to put in a request with Snippet or CreateSpace at whatever point your work is bought. They'll custom print your book and handle stockpiling and satisfaction.

You can make and distribute books on Amazon Kindle Direct Publishing (KDP).

Why Distribute A Book?
1. Why even bother with composing something, assuming there's nobody around to understand it? Independently publishing is the fastest method for getting your book under the control of possible perusers.
2. Printing, stockpiling, and conveyance are dealt with thanks to administrations like Snippet and CreateSpace.
3. Exploratory writing is your obsession, and you should have the option to bring in cash while accomplishing something you appreciate.

Key Action Item: *Utilize your specialized mastery to compose reports and manuals.*

20. Resume And Introductory Letter Writer

Nearly everybody has sought help from others while composing resumes or introductory letters. Offer your mastery in convincing resumes and introductory letters to anyone who can recruit you. Give instances of not simply others' resumes and introductory letters with which you've helped, yet fruitful continues and introductory letters of your own to build your opportunities to begin an internet-based business effectively.

Key Action Item: *Assist with jobbing searchers by supporting them with the ideal continues and introductory letters recorded as a hard copy.*

21. Corporate Direction Advisor

Partnerships need attorneys to safeguard them in lawful matters and teach them what they should or shouldn't do. By beginning a web-based corporate direction conference firm, you can offer corporate laborers a method for keeping their legitimate issues together without extravagant expenses and the broad in-person responsibilities of customary attorneys. You'll have to show evidence that you've produced passing results for the final law test to construct customers and clarify that your business is completely on the web – because when it comes time for your client to go to court, they'll have to recruit a legal counsellor in their locale who can address them before an appointed authority or jury.

Key Action Item: *Offer reasonable, legitimate administrations as a corporate direction specialist.*

22. Startup Guide

Many of the world's most noticeable tech organizations started as new little companies sorting out the right action plan for progress. As a startup guide, you can encourage the upcoming organizations today. Utilize your ability in corporate money, programming advancement and other pertinent fields to give new organizations the information they need to succeed. As these novel companies succeed, your business would do likewise.

Key Action Item: *If you've excelled at starting a business, help others start theirs.*

23. Begin Your Dress Line

You can get your dress organization going if you have a few plans as the main priority and a smidgen of time to burn. If you own a Shopify store, you can set up your dress line utilizing Printify, Printful, or a comparative item obtaining an application. Each naturally interfaces your store to attire printers and dressmakers. They likewise handle each step of the retail satisfaction process for you, allowing you to plan and transport many pieces right out of the entryway.

Why Start a Dress Line?
1. There's nothing more accomplishing than producing items that individuals will utilize consistently.

2. When you fabricate your Shopify store, you'll have the option to begin selling immediately. Because of print-on-request applications, the method involved with planning and conveying your own specially crafted clothing has been smoothed out and streamlined.
3. You'll cherish seeing your plans become completely awake by changing your imagination into something genuine and productive.
4. We utilized Printful to make THINK Little guy, a clothing store for canine proprietors and made more than $1,200 in only three weeks. With a little time and exploration, you could also be well en route to building an effective shirt organization.

24. **Sell Your Craft On The Web**

Whether you're a painter, picture taker, or performer, there are many internet-based business thoughts and ways of transforming your most recent work of art into a wellspring of income with a flawlessly planned online business site. If artistic creation or photography is your strong point, you can sell your work as prints, materials, and outlined banners utilizing Printify or Printful.

This is a phenomenal method for transforming your specialty into something substantial that individuals can bring back home and incorporate into their space. Is music your thing? You can sell your beats, melodies, tests, and more as computerized downloads.

Investigate The Drum Agent, the biggest web-based drum test business on the planet. It made an effective and maintainable private company model with the assistance of applications like FetchApp and ShipStation.

Why Sell Your Specialty?

1. You'll be important to individuals' lives by getting your work into clients' homes.
2. You'll create a stage for displaying your work by settling on the web.

3. As a craftsman, making crafts isn't simply a side interest — it's a lifestyle. This is your opportunity to transform your enthusiasm into a revenue source and possibly live the dream and get paid for the privilege.

25. **Turn Into An Independent Essayist, Fashioner, Or Engineer**

Essayists, visual planners, and engineers can begin a minimal-expense business because of their gifts. As a specialist, you'll have the option to effectively utilize your abilities by assisting individuals worldwide with their ventures (while bringing in some cash, obviously).

Outsourcing means focusing on something other than months-long undertakings that destroy your available energy. With a manageable stretch, you can get reduced undertakings that fit your timetable.

To find individuals needing your assistance, take a stab at outsourcing commercial centers, such as Upwork and Fiverr.

Significantly, Fiverr is somewhat different from a conventional work-board. As the name proposes, a great deal of the posted positions pays $5. The way to bring in huge cash on Fiverr is cautiously setting up your offers so you can undoubtedly upsell the client for more cash.

For example, you could propose to compose a 150-word presentation for a blog entry as your underlying $5 administration. You could charge another $10 for 150 extra words as an upsell. You can change your administrations until you've found a combo that makes it worth your time and energy.

Make a Shopify store if you need complete command over the amount you charge. You can list your administrations as items and cripple transporting since you will not genuinely convey anything to your clients.

You could utilize applications like BookThatApp and Occasions Schedule to give your clients a choice to plan arrangements.

Why Independent?

1. At the point when you are independent, you pick which projects you need to deal with and set your timetable and working environment.
2. Getting compensated to accomplish something great is a remunerating feeling, whether you're hoping to strike out all alone or need to make additional money toward the end of the week.
3. If you're new to composing, planning, or creating, outsourcing is a phenomenal method for building your portfolio and getting genuine involvement with many ventures. You could find that you have a skill or enthusiasm for something you never anticipated.

26. **Turn Your Secondhand Store Finds**

If you love hitting up secondhand shops and chasing down amazing gives, one extraordinary internet business thought is to put your recycled treasures for sale on the web.

Your prospective customers need to buy cool stuff; moreover, they would rather not dig through old soccer shirts and plaited belts to get their hands on that one astounding find. Exploit this by situating yourself as a dependable guardian who can go out and uncover those incredible rare pieces for other people.

Why Place Your Secondhand Store Finds For Sale?
1. Can we be real for a minute? You'd go over secondhand shop racks in any case,

    so you should bring in some cash while you do it by giving your shopping fixation something to do.
2. The edges are tremendous. Did you track down that $2 RadioShack baseball hat at the end of the week? You can transform it into a $40 classic cap.
3. You're selling something special. No place else on the web can individuals track down the classic assortments that you set up.

27. Take A Shot At Being A Powerhouse

Powerhouse showcasing has detonated on the advertising scene, and moreover clients are turning out to be more sagacious, there are still a lot of business potential chances to be had. Since powerhouses have gotten in steaming hot water for exploitative practices, there's been a development toward miniature forces to be reckoned with — profiles with more modest yet drawn-in followings. Uplifting news: you needn't bother with many devotees to bring in cash on Instagram.

For What Reason Should It Be A Powerhouse?

1. It's a chance to get a prologue to showcasing — especially important if you're keen on chasing after that as a vocation or extra undertaking.
2. You'll find out about new and fascinating brands. You could find items and organizations you love that you could never have found had they not requested your administrations.
3. It's so natural a monkey can make it happen. Indeed, not in a real sense — however, you can make your pet the star if you're camera bashful.

28. Curate Membership Boxes

Membership boxes are themed bundles of different items. There are membership confines in basically every industry, from feast prep units and specialty snacks to wellness items and cosmetics. You can arrange membership boxes around essentially any topic of your decision.

Bokksu, for instance, curates Japanese tidbits and sends them to clients every month.

When you curate membership boxes, you work with brands and artisans to buy and exchange their items in a packaged contribution. Regularly, buyers hope to be astonished by what's in the crate. However, there are some (like dinner prep units) where the client picks what they get.

Why Curate Membership Boxes?
1. It's a feasible occasional business. Incidentally, "membership" boxes are bought as presents more frequently than for the actual purchaser. So if you're just keen on maintaining your web-based business for part of the year, this could be a model worth looking at.
2. It's a developing industry. Membership trade deals developed from $16 billion every 2019 to nearly $28 billion in 2021.
3. You don't have to make your items. All things being equal, you can utilize demonstrated, fruitful items and essentially set them up in a decent bundle.

29. **Put Resources Into Land**

It could sound startling when you hear it; however, putting resources into land is relatively easy to break into whenever you've done all necessary investigations. Contingent upon the market, getting your hands on open doors like available FHA credits can be the launch you want to guarantee a money-streaming business all along.

You don't need to stress over loading stock or production network inconveniences with the land. All things being equal, you can scout properties from the solace of your loveseat. There are startup expenses and buy necessities to represent; however, you can get credits to assist with covering them.

The income you lay out with your most memorable property can be reinvested into purchasing your next. Do this enough times, and you can begin making some serious income numbers.

Why Put Resources Into Land?
1. It's a drawn-out interest in a business with valuing resources and practically prompt income.
2. Land will continuously be popular as a need instead of only a need.

3. It tends to be somewhat distant with the perfect administration structure set up.

30. Sell In Commercial Centers

The capacity to sell your merchandise in commercial centers has been around for a while. However, it's as yet an exceptionally worthwhile method for beginning a maintainable web-based business. Dealer stages like eBay, Treasure trove, Etsy, Offerup, or Facebook Commercial center make the method involved with posting items, catching contact data, and getting instalments simple. The greatest aspect? These monstrous vender stages previously accompanied worked in rush hour gridlock. As the vendor, you must get vital with your posting and monitor what sells and how well you can improve your endeavors. You can do all of this from the solace of your home.

Why Sell In Commercial Centers?
1. It's reasonable to begin without powerful, forthright speculation.
2. You gain admittance to a pool of traffic you probably won't have the option to take advantage of on different stages.
3. The web-based selling abilities you gain can convert into contiguous organizations not too far off.

31. Turn Into An Interpreter

Realizing beyond what one language can make you cash. Alongside web access and a PC, you can be well en route to beginning an internet-based interpretation business. The interpretation business is blasting — it multiplied in size somewhat recently.

As an interpreter, you can apply your abilities to decipher content, gatherings, list of qualifications, books, or even web-based meetings. You can constantly charge or buy the venture as you refine your abilities.

Either way or the other, an interpretation business can be adaptable and rewarding once you get everything rolling with your initial few clients.

Why Start An Interpretation Business?

1. There are a lot of interpretation stages, as Gengo is ready to pay seriously for your abilities on the off chance that you would rather not start your business alone.
2. On the other hand, it's not difficult to list your interpretation administrations on stages like UpWork for a more free way to deal with an interpretation where you can set your costs.
3. Interpretation can be an adaptable business that doesn't need promotion to the board or managing stock.

32. **Begin A Bookkeeping Or Accounting Firm**

Exploit the rising business sector interest in bookkeeping and accounting by going independent and offering your administrations to clients hoping to re-appropriate this piece of their business. The more experience and training you have in the field, the better your odds of coming out on top.

You can bootstrap a bookkeeping or accounting business with admittance to programming like QuickBooks, some informal, and some perseverance. As you gain clients and convey extraordinary work, reference clients come in your direction. As a help-based business, the hardest part about beginning a bookkeeping or accounting adventure is getting everything rolling.

Why Start A Bookkeeping Or Accounting Business?

1. It's an extraordinary method for using your number-related abilities while utilizing the adaptability of working for yourself.
2. You needn't bother many clients to create feasible pay yearly.
3. A help-based efficient bookkeeping and accounting blossom with building connections and returning clients, which makes the computerized showcasing part of the business more sensible.

33. **Turn Into An Internet-based Wellness Coach**

Wellness coaches like Kayla Itsines make huge profits online through enrollments, wellness applications, and digital books. If you're normally capable of being dynamic, beginning a web-based wellness business may be an easy decision.

As you get everything rolling, remember to use online entertainment — wellness is a visual industry. Being available on stages like Instagram and TikTok can be an incredible method for building a crowd of people and winning clients. With a computerized wellness business, you can likewise make a few floods of pay that can be set up latently (think computerized manuals or PDFs of exercise plans).

Why Start A Web-based Wellness Coach Business?
1. There is now a current interest in individuals needing assistance with their wellness process.
2. It should be in every way possible on the web. If you would rather not, you never need to meet individuals for wellness preparation.
3. You can make evergreen 7substance-like courses, cookbooks, or wellness designs that can keep on acquiring income behind the scenes and require insignificant upkeep.

34. Make And Sell NFTs

Making and selling NFTs is one of the most current ways of beginning an internet-based business. An enthusiastic specialty market is worth taking advantage of if you influence local area construction and figure out how to sell NFTs on stages like OpenSea.

If you're a craftsman and now making actual crafts, interpreting those abilities into attractive NFTs can end up being a strong turn into the web-based business world.

To begin with, get educated on what NFTs are, where their worth truly lies, and what instruments you want to get everything rolling, creating NFT craft on the Blockchain and fostering a brand.

Why Make and Sell NFTs?
1. The NFT business is blasting, with a market cap of more than $40 billion, and does not indicate halting.
2. It's incredibly simple to begin and mint your NFTs once you gain proficiency with the fundamentals.
3. It's a strong method for utilizing your innovative abilities and producing pay as you tap into a more extensive computerized crowd.

35. Accomplish Voiceover Work

You can turn into a voiceover artisan from the solace of your home whenever you've fabricated a voiceover that brand makers can trust. Who knows what you can voiceover after you've set up your home recording station?

You can voiceover book recordings, YouTube recordings, web plugs, online classes, coursework, and others. Consider recording a demo reel, laying out an expert site, and laying out a web-based entertainment presence that will draw in potential voiceover clients to you.

Remember that the voiceover business is imaginative, implying you should be innovative in drawing in clients and producing income. Voiceover guides like these can assist you with the beginning.

Why Start A Voiceover Business?
1. Beginning a voiceover business can be a special opportunity for an up-and-comer with the right abilities.
2. It has top-level salary potential depending on how things are utilized.
3. It very well may be an unusual method for bringing cash into an industry that isn't oversaturated.

36. Turn Into A Promotion Expert

Promotions are all over the place. Why not be the person who will make a counselling expense from organizations hoping to enhance their promotion methodology? Yes, that is a business you can run completely on the web.

Promotion advisors like Monica Louie are, as of now, getting it done (and doing it competently!).

What is it that you want to get everything rolling? The conspicuous advances apply here. Pick the sorts of promotions you need to spend significant time in — whether PPC advertisements on Google, Instagram, Facebook, TikTok, or even showcase promotions — and afterwards begin advertising your administrations with an expert site and different help offering bundles.

Remember that counselling is only a great fit for some. You need to have a lot of involvement added to your repertoire to guarantee you can convey results to the clients looking for your promotion skill. If you're fresh out of the plastic, I'm new to promotion methodology, and you should hold off on counselling until you acquire insight.

Why Start A Promotion Counseling Business?
1. What you charge for a promotion counselling business can be adaptable and profoundly reliant upon saw esteem.
2. It's an incredible internet-based business thought if you're canny with individuals, the board, and meeting KPIs.
3. Assuming that you appreciate organizing, it's one of the most outstanding ways of acquiring counselling clients.

37. **Construct Specialty Sites**

The main impediment remaining among you and building specialty sites as a help-based business is an expectation to learn and adapt. Not only are there lots of free online assets you can take advantage of to get familiar with the intricate details of web advancement, but you can also likewise learn web designer stages like Shopify to acquire attractive abilities clients are effectively searching for.

While figuring out how to assemble specialty sites isn't hard, it's the promoting part that could take more legwork. Consider finding your most memorable modest bunch of clients on stages like UpWork, To be sure, or

Fiverr. As you kick things off, remember to gather tributes from past clients so offering your administrations to new clients becomes simpler.

Why Start A Specialty Site Business?
1. There are very little to no startup expenses to get everything rolling in a popular help industry.
2. You can cut the time you spend making specialty sites in half once you make reusable site layouts.
3. Building specialty sites can be a drawing in the undertaking, assuming you have an eye for a plan.

38. **Begin An Enrollment People Group**

Might you at any point say repeating regularly scheduled instalments? That is the exact thing a participation business can accomplish for you. Enrollment business thoughts are boundless.

You can set content behind a paywall or make an individual's just local area that consistently gains admittance to your specialty mastery. Look at enrollment networks like Pinnacle Independent or Superpath for motivation.

As you settle on an enrollment plan of action, get clear on your incentive. You can convey esteem as composed content, video content, selective gathering training, PDFs, guides, courses, or downloadable exercise manuals. It's likewise conceivable to give a month-to-month actual item to every part — however, remember this implies managing mailing, above costs, and stock operations.

Why Start A Participation Business?
1. Participation is an incredible action plan because of the repetitive month-to-month pay potential.
2. You can use the form once-sell-on-numerous occasions model to content creation that the product makes conceivable.

3. There are a lot of out-of-the-container participation creation devices to kick you off rapidly fabricating a center where clients can make their profiles and consume your substance.

39. Advance Supported Posts On Instagram

Instagram accounts in a wide range of specialties are making bank through sponsorships. Here is a speedy once-over of how it functions:

1. Grow an Instagram page in a pertinent industry that fits sponsorships. Accounts like Mochi In The City and Studio Do-It-Yourself are extraordinary instances of this.

2. Make sure you develop a drew-in crowd that connects with your substance.
3. Create a brand pack and contact potential accomplices to examine cooperation.
4. Set your costs, distribute your supported substance, and get compensated.
5. Rinse and rehash.

Why Start An Instagram Sponsorship Business?
1. You needn't bother with cash, confirmations, or clients to get everything rolling.
2. Instagram sponsorships can be a reasonable business that doesn't need to require hours of your time.
3. You can become your Instagram profile naturally without putting forthright cash into showcasing.

HOW WOULD YOU STARTUP AN EFFECTIVE INTERNET BUSINESS?

Beginning a web-based business can be invigorating; however, that doesn't imply it's simple in every case. For instance, there are a few legitimate advances you want to take to begin your business, such as picking your business name, procuring a government manager recognizable proof number (FEIN), deciding your lawful construction and guaranteeing your business. Although each business is novel, you can follow a couple of moves toward expanding your possibility of beginning a fruitful web-based business:

1. Choose a business thought or industry because of your insight and enthusiasm.
2. Find a business specialty in light of holes in the commercial center.
3. Conduct statistical surveying and cutthroat investigation to evaluate your opposition and item reasonability.
4. Familiarize yourself with the morals and regulations of online organizations. e) Shop around before picking a program to construct your web-based store.
5. Create an extensive promoting methodology (e.g., site, email showcasing, Search engine optimization, web-based entertainment advertising, nearby advertising, and so forth.)

Key Action Item: Distinguish a market hole and begin an internet-based business by observing the vital web-based business regulations.

THE MOST EFFECTIVE METHOD TO BEGIN A WEB-BASED BUSINESS IS IN 6 STAGES.

Whenever you've settled on an internet-based business thought, you'll believe that it should take care of any outstanding concerns and, at last, give it life. This is the way to begin a business on the web, bit by bit:

1. **Approve Your Thought With Exploration**

It could sound brutal. Yet, at the same it's valid: because you assume you have an extraordinary thought, that doesn't mean there's a business opportunity for it. Before investing in your business, research how possible it is and whether there's any potential purchaser premium.

You can recruit an office to lead statistical surveying for you, yet on the off chance that you're on a tight spending plan, you can adopt the Do-It-Yourself strategy. After directing statistical surveying, compose a marketable strategy to explain your thoughts. Having a field-tested strategy will assist you with remaining coordinated and engaged as you go through the promising and less promising times of beginning another business. If you would rather not start a business without preparation, you can continuously purchase a current business with approved thoughts.

2. **Foster Your Item Or Administration**

You've approved your thought. Presently it is the ideal time to transform it into a reality. Whether you're selling an item or administration, you want to make it.

Track down a producer to rejuvenate your item, make bundles of your administration contributions, or compose your book and recognize an independent publishing choice to carry it to completion. If you go to the outsourcing course, I previously created the item for you. It depends on you to pick the items you're enthusiastic about or that you've recognized a hot market for.

3. **Set Up Your Business Funds**

"How would I open a business financial balance?" is a typical inquiry for most new business visionaries. After you've formally enlisted your business with your neighborhood government, you ought to have the duty recognizable proof numbers and other data expected to start a business financial balance. As you develop, you could require financing for future undertakings, be it another item sent off or showcasing and publicizing spend. Having business financial balances makes it simpler for you to deal with that capital and track your income and costs. A ledger is likewise useful regarding burden planning since your business-related exchanges will be in a solitary spot. As your business funds get more confounded, employing an expert bookkeeper or expense proficient could be a practical choice.

4. Track Down Merchants And Providers

Item-Based Web-based organizations specifically may require heaps of business connections. For instance: a maker, a dropshipper, or an outsider strategies facilitator. While distinguishing which associations you need to push ahead with, it's ideal to look around and contrast your choices to ensure you get the best answer for your necessities. Other web-based business thoughts might require various connections or workers for hire. For instance, if you're composing a book, you might need to recruit an expert proofreader and book originator.

5. Construct Your Business Site

If you desire to begin an internet-based business, you want to have a site. Furthermore, you'll have to consolidate instalment handling usefulness to bring in cash on the web. In the first place, find a business name.

You can utilize a business name generator to help concoct one if you're stuck. You'll require one to begin constructing your site. Then, at that point, pick a space name and confirm that it's accessible. You can sometimes buy a space name for under $20 a year. From that point, you can construct your store on a stage like Shopify and begin tolerating instalments from clients immediately.

6. Market Your New Private Company

Getting your most memorable paying client is a colossal achievement for another entrepreneur. Now that your store is set up, you'll need to get your business out there. Be that as it may, tracking down new clients and making persuading advancements takes investment. There are countless channels to browse — email advertising, Courier showcasing, portable promoting, and so forth — it isn't easy to know the ideal way to develop your web-based business. It's not difficult to become involved with some unacceptable strategies and put your time and cash in some unacceptable spots.

BEGIN YOUR WEB-BASED BUSINESS TODAY!

If you've been pondering beginning a web-based business, now is the right time to get out there and make your new startup in your extra time. You don't need to bet on everything. Begin a little with a part-time side gig and scale from that point. Or, on the other hand, keep things little. The excellence of figuring out how to begin a business online is that it's dependent upon you.

ONLINE BUSINESS THOUGHTS FAQ

How Would You Conceptualize Online Business Thoughts?
1. Make a conceptualizing board and put every one of your thoughts on it.
2. Return with new thoughts and refine your rundown.
3. Find support from loved ones.
4. Overview existing clients to track down new internet-based business thoughts.
5. Check search patterns on Google Patterns. And so on.

What Is The Best Internet-based Business From Start's perspective? Or What Sort Of Online Business Is Generally Beneficial?

Out of the web-based business types above, corporate direction counselling is the most generously compensated, trailed by application improvement. Some experts in web-based organizations also anticipate instructive cooperation's - mentoring, computerized courses, YouTube channels and even Skype training - to obtain higher benefits for subsequent years, with online business destinations following a bit close in benefits. In the interim, others are: *Outsourcing | A Dress Line | Selling Craftsmanship | Organizing Membership Boxes | Selling Hand-tailored Products | Being An Offshoot Advertiser | A Blog | A Counselling Business Etc.*

Key Focus Point: *Corporate guidance counselling and programming advancement are among the most productive internet-based organizations.*

What Is The Best Web-based Business To Begin From Home?

A Web-based Business Store | Purchasing Items In Mass To Sell Online | Teaching Web-based Courses | A Composing Business | Online Administrations
| Selling Handcrafted Items | Beginning A YouTube Channel | Turning Into A Blogger. And so forth.

What Are Some Internet-based Service Business Thoughts?

Graphic Design | Independent Composition | Wordpress Development | Shopify Topic Building | Application Development | Website Composition | Copywriting | Site Design Development Counselling.

How Would I Begin A Little Web-based Business?

1. Find a hole in a specialty market and fill it
2. Figure out how to compose a duplicate that sells
3. Assemble and plan your site
4. Get via virtual entertainment destinations like Instagram, Facebook, and LinkedIn
5. Streamline your site for Website optimization
6. Turn into a specialist in your industry
7. Give amazing client assistance
8. Make various types of revenue.

Do I Want An LLC To Sell On The Web?

You needn't bother with an LLC to sell on the web, yet it's suggested that you document for one. As an entrepreneur, this mitigates risk and safeguards your own resources on the off chance you end up in a claim or need financial protection.

THE CASE FOR CLARITY

Before the advanced age, just a special minority could unite the assets important to go into business. Beginning capital must be critical, while outside subsidizing was in many cases scant except if you had associations with monetary and pioneering know-how. That is not true in online deals and online business, as the interest in web-based business and online organizations has detonated. Indeed, even over the most recent couple of years, internet business development has been gigantic. From 2019 to 2021, web-based business deals developed over half, addressing 13.2% of all retail ventures in the U.S.

Today, anybody can begin and scale an internet-based business, paying little heed to the proficient foundation or past pioneering experience.
In any case, while the passage hindrance has been brought down, it's not gone. Potential entrepreneurs must foster a quality item thought, sort out obtaining or producing procedure and execute a feasible deals model.

REASONS YOU OUGHT TO BEGIN AN INTERNET-BASED BUSINESS

You might be wondering, why start a web-based business in any case? Why not go with a physical one, all things being equal?

The response? Beginning a web-based business enjoys a few benefits, including:

1. **It Is Genuinely Reasonable To Begin**

Many need to begin a business, yet are prevented by the venture expected to get it going. You should pay for rent, buy stock, and financial plan for representative pay rates. On the off chance that the business fizzles, it could demolish you monetarily.
In any case, with a web-based business, all you want is the following:

1. PC.
2. Space Name.
3. Web Designer.

Sending off an internet-based business with $100 as a beginning capital is plausible. You don't have to put your life in danger's reserve funds to become a fruitful web-based business visionary.

1. **Outstanding Prospective And Development**

When you have a physical business, you need to manage the limits of this present reality, from land expenses to nearby interest.

At the point when you manage an internet business, none of these limits apply. You can offer to anyone — regardless of where they reside, and with every year — your pool of potential clients grows because more individuals are becoming familiar with web-based shopping.

By 2025, online businesses will represent almost 25% of worldwide retail deals. Moreover, the world wide web populace is likewise developing as they project web clients to reach 5.6 billion by 2025.

More individuals online mean more likely openness for your internet-based brand — particularly if you wouldn't fret about taking your web-based business across the line.

2. **Continuously On**

Another online benefit organizations have over physical organizations is that they can remain open every minute of every day, even through lockdowns and different interruptions.

When your business is on the web, you are widely accessible to make a transaction. Customers can arrange from you whenever.

Since you needn't be truly present to make a deal, your business can produce income with less everyday inclusion.

3. **Decide Your Specialty And Business Thought**

A business specialty is your center region — a market portion and ideal interest group you fundamentally take care of. This can be anybody, from sports fans to specialists to experts.

You want to make a specialization for your new business. To track down the right interest group, guarantee they have:
1. An issue no other person is settling.
2. Eagerness to pay for an answer to that issue.
3. Appropriate optional pay to maintain the cost of the organization.

Clarity As A Business Perspective

We experience a daily reality such that information breaks are going on at an outrageous rate, counterfeit news is posted all over, and deception is typical.

That might sound a little doomsayer, yet it's valid. The computerized age has brought numerous individuals web-based, making humanity more associated than whenever in our set of experiences. There are 7.7 individuals possessing planet Earth, and 3.5 billion of us are on the web! The web has without a doubt brought us numerous extraordinary things and changed how we live to improve things. We presently approach a tremendous abundance of data with a couple of taps of the fingers. Extravagant sites, innovative programming, and an enormous reach are at this point not only for the goliath associations with colossal income—it's for everybody.

AI and computer-based intelligence have impelled us into another time of innovation. Besides the fact that we getting increasingly more are strong projects, our admittance to them is expanding too. The web is to a great extent, liable for this. The abundance of data on the web and developing paces of web access have permitted gifted individuals all around the globe to add to the aggregate human information. These individuals might have recently been cut off from this world because of an absence of schooling and different boundaries. Trend-setting innovation and a higher populace of talented individuals remain closely connected and lead to where we are today. Anyway, where could we today be? In this present reality where cutting-edge programming is available, modest, and for organizations of all sizes.

Be that as it may, with every one of the extraordinary things the web has given us, there's likewise some awful. At the point when everybody has simple admittance to making and sharing data, the drawback is that there's a ton of inaccurate data out there. This leads individuals to have general doubts about the substance they read on the web. This doubt likewise gets applied to organizations where individuals are hesitant to believe organizations that need straightforwardness. If an organization isn't straightforward and clear about its practices and objectives, then individuals stress that they are concealing something. This secret something could be unfortunate strategic policies or issues with items, and the sky is the limit from there.

Client assumptions for straightforwardness are developing. It's likewise a fact that being more clear and more straightforward will straightforwardly affect your deals. One investigation discovered that 85% of Americans are bound to stay by a business in a brand emergency, assuming the organization has a background marked by being straightforward. We're currently where lucidity is certainly not a pleasure to have, it's an unquestionable requirement!
Considering this, we should investigate why clients expect lucidity and straightforwardness and how you can work on these in your business.

Why Clients Anticipate Clarity

1. *Trust In Your Business*

Buyers will close off organizations that don't satisfy their guidelines of lucidity and straightforwardness. This comes down to trust. Organizations with unfortunate straightforwardness and indistinct objectives and practices are viewed as conniving.

As a business, it ought to be the main concern to win the trust of your clients. Keep in mind, without your clients, your business wouldn't exist.

Cheerful clients are your best advertising procedure and clients are more joyful with organizations they can trust. Cheerful clients will tell their loved ones, they'll compose surveys for you on the web, and follow you via virtual entertainment. All of this adds to your image character. If you can keep these clients, and keep them cheerful, you'll draw in additional clients. In any case, it's likewise a fact that troubled clients educate individuals concerning their experience as well. Around 13% of miserable clients tell over 20 individuals. That is, 20 additional individuals on the planet presently got some distance from your business because of trust. They trust their loved ones, and their cherished one has no faith in them.

Notwithstanding, you can involve a troubled client as a potential chance to construct trust. How you treat despondent clients can make a huge difference, and the way into this change is clarity and straightforwardness. You want to draw in your troubled clients and ask them for what valid reason they are miserable.

Just 1 out of 28 despondent clients will gripe straightforwardly to you. This implies you have possibly many miserable clients strolling the roads and you're ignorant about it. It's fundamental to use your client care group to pose significant inquiries about consumer loyalty and client experience.

Trust runs past your clients, it likewise reaches out to your expected financial backers. If your business has a culture of concealing things away or limiting admittance to data, or correspondence, this will cause your business to seem dishonest.

2. Brand Character

Buyers are presently savvier in recent memory and tracking down an elective organization to work with should be possible effortlessly. There's a gigantic measure of strain to have high client standards for dependability, yet it's definitely worth the work you cut in. Simply expanding your client standards for dependability by 7% can build your benefits by 30% to 92%.

In light of that, it couldn't be more obvious why developing customer dependability is an unquestionable prerequisite. One way that you develop client dependability is through areas of strength for honesty. You do this by giving a steady encounter, keeping an open line of correspondence with your clients, and staying up with the latest with what's going on in your business.

3. *Purchasing Certainty*

Lucidity in business reaches out past the domain of general straightforward practices and into how you address your items and administrations. Are applicable insights regarding your items and administrations recorded on your site in a simple-to-understand way? Do your clients know precisely the exact thing they're getting from you? Does your client care group realize the items are all right to address any question tossed at them? These are questions you ought to get some information about your business.

There are countless choices accessible and customers, and the most recent examination recommends that cutting-edge purchasers favor accommodation.

This intends that if your site is muddled and cumbersome to utilize, and there's an absence of correspondence channels open to the purchaser, they will take their cash somewhere else.

The Significance Of Clarity

All organizations will encounter deals that fail to work out, items that lemon, colleagues that don't play out their job well, etc. In any case, the light of the fact that these situations might be once in a while unavoidable doesn't mean you ought to pause for a minute and allow them to occur. Such numerous business directors chalk these situations down to outside conditions, accepting there is no hope, yet this is bogus. The absence of clarity is much of the time the issue.

You should have a reasonable comprehension of the business and have the option to speak with lucidity to your clients. There are two or three methods for encouraging this climate of clarity:

> ***Utilize Clear And Compact Correspondences With Clients:*** A few clients lack the opportunity to peruse endlessly pages of item data, all things considered. You should list item all that they need to be aware of and make short notes.
> ***Incorporate Straightforwardness Into Your Business:*** Utilize the furthest down-the-line innovation to offer a more direct encounter to your clients. Clients will battle to keep an unmistakable mentality if their current circumstance isn't clear. Assuming the devices and programming utilized are all siloed and client information is challenging to determine, they will battle. An omnichannel way to deal with client care is an enormous advantage here. Having each of your representatives working from one comprehensive stage prompts a more profound and more clear comprehension of the clients and the business. This will then, at that point, emphatically affect the client experience.

Advantages of Focusing on Clarity

1. Teem Client Retention

If a client has purchased from you once previously, you've proactively done the crucial step. With shopping basket relinquishment rates across all businesses being more than 70%, this part is no simple accomplishment. If a client purchases from you two times, you can feel sure that their most memorable experience lived up to their assumptions. Nonetheless, you ought to never be too certain concerning the soul of your business; clients, and the cash they part with. Clients care about the three Cs: comfort, clarity, and consistency. If a client begins to have a befuddled outlook on your business and what you are offering, they'll escape. The equivalent is valid assuming that they find it hard to purchase from your business. If they had a smooth course of getting one item, the equivalent ought to be valid for any remaining buys.

2. **Propagate Client Acquisition**

As we've quite recently examined, switching a likely client over completely to a completely fledged client is the critical step. This is where separating yourself from the group is significant. You want to demonstrate your value to your clients through your strategic policies. Here are a few fast tips:

- ➤ ***Be Fundamentally Straightforward And Forthright:*** Tell your clients precisely the thing they're getting. You can incorporate a straightforward list item rundown of particulars for your item first and afterward add a long attempt to close the deal. Time is an important product in the cutting-edge world and only one out of every odd has the opportunity and willpower to analyze what you offer, so don't make them.
- ➤ ***Permit, However, Two-way Discourse With Clients As Could Reasonably Be Expected:*** It's presently not satisfactory to simply offer a telephone number as the main method for correspondence. Clients presently hope to have the option to speak with organizations in their particular manner.

  More youthful shoppers predominantly really like to utilize Live Visit benefits. Certain individuals will like to call, others email, and others are cheerfully conversing with a chatbot.

  Anything that the inclination, ensure you take care of it. The equivalent goes for the hours of the day your business is open for this correspondence. Simply working between the customary working hours is presently not satisfactory either – clients need all-day, everyday access, or as near this as they can get.

3. ***Expansion In Deals***

This one is basic. An expansion in client securing and client maintenance prompts more deals and higher benefits for your organization.

3 MOVES TOWARD MAKING AND KEEPING UP WITH CLIENT LUCIDITY

1. **No Secret Expenses Or Astonishments**

Lucidity is tied in with guaranteeing your client grasps the start-to-finish cycle of managing your organization. There ought to be no curve balls or secret costs that dismiss them or leave them feeling tricked later down the line.

The main justification for shopping basket relinquishment is additional costs that are excessively high, with 55% of customers saying for this reason they deserted their shopping basket. 21% of the customer additionally said they deserted their shopping basket because they couldn't see the absolute expense, and 17% said it was because they have zero faith in the site.

2. **Share News And Updates With Clients And Request Criticism**

Obviously, you shouldn't spam your clients with many messages, however very much planned, and it is an unquestionable necessity to draw in correspondence. If you're making changes in your business, let your clients know. If you have another item emerging, let them know. At the point when you've made changes, ask your clients for input on their client experience.

If you don't ask how your clients feel, you won't ever know how to get to the next level.

3. **Be Accessible**

If that a client or potential client has inquiries regarding your business, you ought to be accessible to respond to them and answer rapidly. Indeed, even organizations with good motivations will accidentally make confounding interchanges, yet how you answer issues emerge that is significant. A little disaster can develop into a major issue if you don't answer rapidly, so answering rapidly is an unquestionable requirement.

Executing rehearses around lucidity and straightforwardness will emphatically affect your benefit. Trust in the data we get is at an untouched low so buyers esteem genuineness, uprightness, straightforwardness, and clarity like never before previously. Thusly, you ought to focus on lucidity for your business. Set up a culture of clarity inside your business through the innovation you use, how you treat and train your representatives, and how you speak with clients.

DEVELOP YOUR BUSINESS.

There has never been a superior opportunity to construct a business selling on the web courses. By 2027, the worldwide e-learning market is assessed to come to a gigantic $521.8 billion (Exploration and Markets), flagging a colossal

potential. A great many individuals are buying web courses, inside and beyond the conventional schooling system, to overhaul their insight and abilities. It shocks no one that because of this interest, business people and informed authorities from everywhere the world have begun making and offering web courses to impart their insight to other people. Be that as it may, we should be genuine here.

Assuming you inquire as to whether it was simple for them to construct their business, they will let you know that it wasn't. Rome wasn't underlying a day, nor is it an internet-based course business. Toward the start of 2017, Smith watched his dear companion open his barbershop. It took him 3 months of remodels and a huge number of dollars just to prepare his barbershop for him to invite his initial client through the front entryway. (I was his subsequent client, coincidentally.

Another person beat Smith to the fantastic opening by around 5 minutes!) For Smith's companion, those 3 months of readiness work were only the start. During the following half year after his great opening, he worked 7 days out of every week to develop his customers and recover his startup costs before he began employing more hairdressers. For what reason did he do this? Since that is what it took to begin his barbershop.

What Does This Have To Do With Building A Web-based Course Business?
The place of this story is that it takes a great deal of work forthright to construct a business. It doesn't come about coincidentally and building an internet-based course business is no special case. There is a ton of work you should do, both when you make your course, and to find true success. Sadly, most course makers abandon their business before investing the effort expected to guarantee they will find lasting success. They quit searching for gold before they experience the huge result that makes all the difficult work worth the effort.

Although it takes a ton of work to construct an effective internet-based course business, there are a lot of others that have done it previously. Because of that, we connected with over 40 fruitful business visionaries and online course makers.

These individuals have in a real sense, fabricated their vocations by imparting their insight to other people, many of them selling a great many dollars' worth of preparing programs and online courses all through their professions.

In the wake of evaluating every one of the important experiences these web-based course creation specialists and business visionaries imparted to us, we figured out how to distill the most common way of incorporating an effective internet-based course business into 8 explicit advances (indeed, more like stages, since every single one of these stages has a few stages included).

8 MOVES TOWARD BUILDING AN EFFECTIVE INTERNET-BASED COURSE BUSINESS

Before we hop into Stage 1, there is something vital that you want to comprehend: without help from anyone else, an internet-based course isn't a business. Without a web-based course to sell, you can't precisely construct an internet-based course business. In any case, making your web-based course is only one piece of building your business. Your internet-based course is your item. It's not your whole business. As may be obvious, an ordinary web-based course business has numerous parts, too.

This might astound you, yet making a web-based course isn't even the most vital phase during the time spent building an internet-based course business. Out of the 8 stages we're going to go through, making a course is Step #6.

You're free to skip stages 1-5 assuming you need to, yet I would exhort against it, and here's the reason: On the off chance that you hop directly to making a course without decisively picking a subject to educate (Stage 1), making a plan of action (Stage 2), and approving interest for that point (Stage 3), you could wind up making a course that nobody needs to pursue.

Furthermore, on the off chance that you don't construct your image (Stage 4) and the crowd (Stage 5) preceding you send off your course, you will not have a method for standing apart among your opposition or have a group of people to elevate your course to.

Regardless of whether you have the "great" course made today, without a convincing brand and a crowd of people to elevate it to, producing sales will be truly challenging. No deals = no business to elevate it to, producing sales will be truly challenging. No deals = no business. So, to save yourself numerous long stretches of exertion and (possibly) huge amount of dollars in course creation and showcasing costs, don't skirt these means.

Bargain? All right, we should make a plunge...

Stage 1: Choose What To Educate
The most important phase in building a web-based course business is concluding what you will educate.

What subject would you like to become known for? What theme would you say you are master to the point of educating other people?

To be a master of something, you simply need to find out more about your point than the individual you are instructing. That is all there is to it. To that individual, you're a specialist. Don't overthink this.

1. Pick Your Course Theme

Between the blend of your background and your expert experience, there are reasons for a few subjects that you know enough about going to make a seminar on.

To assist with reducing a particular course point, we suggest finishing the accompanying activity:

On a piece of paper, define 2 vertical boundaries to make 3 sections. Mark the principal segment Interests and Interests. Mark the second segment Abilities. Name the third section Insight and Accomplishments.

Then, begin adding however many things as you can imagine to every section (go for the gold 20 for each segment).

Whenever you've done this, distinguish the main 2-3 points where your interests/interests, your abilities, and your experience/accomplishments meet. For instance, if you like sci-fi (energy/interest), you're an extraordinary essayist (expertise), and you've composed a few sci-fi books (insight/accomplishment),

then, at that point "how to compose a sci-fi novel" is a feasible subject to think about educating to other people.

"You've been given an ability, you've been given a gift, you've been given encounters in your day-to-day existence that are here to serve others." – Alexi Panos

1. Recognize A Particular Interest Group

Whenever you've recognized a particular subject to educate, the following stage is to distinguish a particular interest group (otherwise known as an objective market) that is keen on that point.

Try not to wrongly believe that your subject (and in this manner, your course) will engage everybody.

Assuming you attempt to make a course that requests everybody, it will probably interest nobody. I know it's nonsensical, however, trust me on this.

To give you a model, one of our clients (Lizzie Lasater) is a yoga professional and educator. At the point when she chose to make online courses, normally, she chose to begin showing yoga on the web.

Rather than making courses to show individuals how to rehearse yoga (an extremely wide and exceptionally serious subject), she chose to limit her ideal interest group to other yoga educators (more unambiguous). With other yoga educators as her ideal interest group, she made courses that are explicitly about how to improve as a yoga instructor.

Stage 2: Make A Marketable strategy For Your Internet Training Business

Whenever you have settled on what to instruct and have adequate clarity about your course theme, the time has come to prepare your strategy. A strategy or plan of action is a conventional diagram depicting how you will structure, oversee and showcase your internet-based course business. It is essential to make one as it assists with guaranteeing that your web-based course business will stay serious and monetarily fruitful in the long haul.

You can pick one of the numerous product instruments to make a standard field-tested strategy or utilize a normal bookkeeping sheet or word-handling programming.

Presently, as each business is unique, their plans of action can differ radically. Be that as it may, certain perspectives stay normal in most organizations. Here, we have spread out what you should remember for your strategy:

1. ***Depict Your Business***

A business depiction is expected to express the motivation behind your business, your interest group, and how you intend to convey your items and administrations.

While drafting it, you should be all around as a goal and compact as conceivable for the idea of your web-based course and how it expects to help the main interest group. Make a point to feature on the off chance that you will convey your courses just on the web or disconnected.

It likewise assists with expressing on the off chance that your courses will be teacher driven or conveyed through other e-learning techniques.

2. Recognize Your Advertising Strategy

When you depict the idea of your business, the subsequent stage is to assemble a promoting and deals technique.

Portray the methodologies you will use to showcase your web-based course and how you intend to execute your email advertising, online entertainment promoting, and other natural techniques.

Moreover, you want to want to designate a spending plan for your paid ads and web-based showcasing on the off chance that you choose to settle on pay-per-click promotion programs.

3. Recruiting And Group Management

While numerous internet-based course makers decide to run their shows, many select to recruit menial helpers or full-time representatives for help. Others decide to appoint errands to consultants or outsider merchants.

Make a point to portray how you intend to designate the undertakings you can't do. It is dependably smart to re-appropriate assignments that don't need your intercession to save time for those that require your aptitude.

4. Business Tasks

This part of the b-plan states how your everyday business exercises will be organized and made due.

You can incorporate your course happy, functional hours, telecom and IT-related necessities, protection, and so on. The more compact your activities segment, the better ground it makes for you to approve your arrangement later.

5. **Funds**

Each business expects cash to run, and online organizations are no exemption. Notwithstanding the promoting and publicizing costs referenced above, you will likewise have to calculate framework, innovation, recruiting, and so forth. Make sure to likewise depict what you intend to sell and how you intend to adapt your business.

With this, try to have a point-by-point financial arrangement and distribute your assets to various costs wisely. In any case, be mindful to guarantee that your financial plan is inside what you can focus on and it doesn't cause you to feel overextended.

Note that notwithstanding your web-based business course, you may likewise add other revenue streams, for example, selling digital books, offering paid talks, and so on.

6. **Two Monetary Estimations You Ought To Think About At First Are:**

Net Overall revenue: This is the number of courses you sell less the expense of running your web-based course. It tends to be addressed as a rate.

Net Overall revenue = (Net course deal incomes—the cost of running your internet-based course)/net course deals x 100

Selling, General, And Authoritative (SG&A) Proportion: This figure lets you know the level of your web-based course deals income used to cover your functional costs.

SGA = [Selling + General + Functional (Managerial) expenses]/Net web-based course deals income

While we have portrayed the fundamental parts of a strategy, it likewise assists with following the design of a conventional Plan of action material. Alexander Osterwalder advocated this idea in 2005 and comprised nine structure blocks. These incorporate key accomplices, exercises, assets, cost structure, income streams, offers, client connections, channels, and client fragments.

Stage 3: Approve Market Interest

Whenever you've distinguished a particular point to educate and have your fundamental marketable strategy diagram set up, the subsequent stage is to approve the interest in that subject.

As a course maker, it sucks to spend a little while, perhaps months (or years?!), making a web-based course about a theme that you figure out there is no interest for.

It's much more productive to approve interest for your course forthright before you contribute time, exertion, and cash to making a course.

The following are 2 different ways you can approve the interest for your course point:

1. Research Your Opposition

Check whether you can find others or organizations that are selling courses and different types of preparation about your point (or a comparable one), or who serve your ideal interest group.

1. Top-of-the-line books on Amazon
2. Other web-based courses
3. Famous online journals and discussions
4. Top web recordings on iTunes
5. In-person courses, meetings, studios
6. Online occasions (virtual highest points, online courses)
7. Organizing bunches on Meetup
8. Mentors and experts.

If you can't find anybody that is productively showing your subject to other people, that is a warning that there isn't sufficient market interest for that point to legitimize making a web-based course (or building a business). Rivalry is generally proof of market interest.

Imagine a scenario in which there is no rivalry?!
In the uncommon event that you can't find any contending items or administrations about your subject, that could mean one of two things:
- There is a request, yet nobody is serving that market yet (intriguing), or
- There is no interest, and you ought to pick an alternate theme

One way or another, there are as yet two additional means you ought to take before you pull the trigger and choose to make (or not make) your course.

An extraordinary method for checking interest in your subject is to utilize Google's Watchword Organizer to perceive the number of individuals that are looking for your point each month. The higher the inquiry volume, the higher the interest.

"Try not to fear rivalry. Their very presence approves that there is an interest for the issue you're attempting to tackle or for an answer for it."
- Greg Smith, Chief of Thinkific

2. Ask Your Main Interest Group What They Need To Realize

If you approach your interest group, whether on the web or disconnected, the most ideal way to figure out what they need to realize (and might want to pay to learn) is to straightforwardly ask them!

The following are a couple of ways you can ask your crowd what they need to realize:
1. Request your rundown from email endorsers
2. Ask your fans/supporters via web-based entertainment
3. Ask your past or potentially existing clients.

ADVANCED INTERNET TYCOONS' SECRETS

With every one of these choices, you can send individuals a connection to a study, ask them unconditional inquiries straightforwardly, or request that they have a speedy call with you.

Another way is an immediate effort (also known as cold pitching) to your ideal interest group by telephone, email, or web-based entertainment. Do this in a respectful, non-malicious method.

Perceive the number of individuals that are looking for your course thoughts on google.

Taking part in catchphrase research is an extraordinary method for distinguishing a course subject that might potentially sell quickly, without straightforwardly asking your crowd.

Catchphrase research assists you with understanding what individuals are searching for online by entering wording on Google or other web search tools.

To lead watchword research on subjects that might intrigue your crowd, you can utilize specific instruments like SEMRush or Ahrefs.

Regardless of the apparatus you decide to use, here is the fundamental system to participate in watchword research:

Recognize your seed term, which would be an umbrella term for your course point.

Type in "course" + your seed term.

Get explicit and find a specialty region that other course makers have not covered but has a high hunt volume. Look at this instrument to recognize search volume.

Proceed to look and dispense with subjects that are not possible or fascinating.

For instance, if you wish to begin a web-based seminar on planting, type "cultivating course" in the watchword search device. You will see various outcomes with various hunt volumes. These outcomes will assist you with getting more unambiguous. For instance, you might see that "cultivating courses in semi-dry districts" is a potential course point with a good hunt volume.

Then again, you can likewise utilize our pursuit volume device to find famous course point thoughts.

Keep in mind: to become familiar with the subject that you're considering educating, you ought to most likely continue toward another point.

If you can't find purchasers before you make your course, you most likely won't find any after by the same token!

The ideal situation is you pick a point that there is an interest for (demonstrated by contending items and administrations about that subject), yet nothing that is for your particular interest group.

Facebook showcasing, for instance, is a wide subject area of strength for the request (demonstrated by each of the websites, books, courses, specialists, workshops, and so on about this point).

Presently, expecting we need to make a course about Facebook showcasing, we should find out what points we think of as we focus on a particular interest group:

- Theme 1: *Facebook Advertising 101 (extremely wide)*
- Theme 2: *Facebook Promoting For Entrepreneurs (More Unambiguous, Still Beautiful And Expansive)*
- Theme 3: *Facebook Promoting For Neighborhood Organizations (Not Terrible)*
- Theme 4: *Facebook Advertising For Realtors (Unmistakable)*
- Theme 5: *Facebook Showcasing Methodologies To Get More Postings (Ding Ding, We Have A Champ!)*

If you are a realtor and you need to figure out how to utilize Facebook to get more postings, which course subject will speak to you the most? Which subject could you pay the most cash for? Likely #5, because it is the most unambiguous. It is the precisely very thing you need to learn.

"The most straightforward method for understanding what to do is stand by listening to what individuals are requesting and afterward give that to them."
- JJ Virgin, VIP Nutritionist, and Wellness Master

Stage 4: Make A Convincing And Special Brand

Whenever you've settled on a particular point to instruct, now is the ideal time to begin constructing your image.

Try not to hop directly to get your logo, site, and business cards planned.

Those things truly do assume a part in addressing your image, yet they are not the beginning stage.

The beginning stage of making a convincing and special brand is coming to a cognizant conclusion about how you need to be situated in your industry.

Branding is tied in with situating. Your image ought to situate you as the go-to master on your point. Except if you're situated as a specialist and a believed expert on your theme, it will be difficult to persuade somebody to purchase a course (or any item or administration) from you.

Although we're told not to, we do make a judgment too quickly. Consider your image as the "book cover" for your business.

1. Be Key With Your Situating

The greatest mix-up that individuals (and associations) make with their marking is attempting to interest everybody. Try not to do that. Be vital in your situating.

Fabricate a brand that requests your particular interest group. Try not to attempt to engage everybody, since everybody isn't your optimal client/client.

Here are a few inquiries to consider as you make your image:

How would you like to be situated and seen in your commercial center? What do you maintain that individuals should consider when they think about you? Whom would you like to draw? Whom would you like to draw? What do you depend on? What do you remain against? For what reason are you and you doing the same thing?

At the point when your ideal interest group is looking for data about your subject, you believe that they should track down you and promptly feel like they've come to the perfect locations. They ought to feel like they've tracked down the specific individual (or organization) that can assist them with beating a particular issue or accomplishing a particular result.

"An extraordinary brand begins with understanding what your identity is, a big motivator for you, grasping your commercial center and figuring out your situating." - Re Perez, Chief of Marking For Individuals

2. Distinguish Your Remarkable Incentive

An activity that we suggest all course makers complete is making An Extraordinary Offer (AEO). Your AEO will assist you with separating yourself from your opposition.

To make your AEO, answer these inquiries:
1. Whom do you help?
2. What do you assist them with doing?
3. Why is that valuable for them?

When you have the responses to these inquiries, integrate them into a solitary sentence.

To give you a model, one of our clients, Ellie Diop, otherwise known as Ellie Talks Cash, is a business mentor with a demonstrated history that assists you with scaling your business and having monetary achievement. Very great AEO right?

As may be obvious, any individual who visits her site will want to immediately sort out what her identity is, what she does, and who her interest group is. She has an unmistakable and convincing individual brand.

If you're somebody who has any desire to work on your business and arrive at monetary achievement, it's conspicuous you've come to the ideal locations.

Great branding causes your main interest group to feel like they've come to the perfect locations.

Stage 5: Form Your Crowd
Whenever you've concluded how you need to be situated in your market, now is the right time to begin constructing your crowd.

Your crowd is the aggregate of the multitude of individuals that you can speak with through different conveyance channels (your blog, web-based entertainment, email list, individual organization, and so on.).

Why Is It Critical To Construct A Group Of People?
Without a crowd of people that knows, like, and trusts you, it will be undeniably challenging to sell your course for the straightforward explanation that you don't have anybody to offer it to!

So the sooner you begin constructing your crowd, the better.

"Online courses are the flood representing things to come. They can assist with extending my substance and message into spots and nations that I still can't seem to visit. Online courses have supported my pay and assisted me with imparting my message to a lot bigger crowd." - Andrea Beaman, Wellbeing Teacher and Creator

1. Instructions to Characterize Your Interest group
It helps if you follow an orderly system to characterize your interest group. Helpful moves toward that end include:
1. Ask your ongoing clients
2. Get subtleties on socioeconomics like age, orientation, area, and so on.
3. Comprehend their requirements and problem areas

4. Investigate the arrangement they're expecting
5. Make a client symbol

2. Size Is Significant (However Not The Most Significant)

The size of your crowd is significant, but not quite as significant as you could naturally suspect. The conspicuous advantage of having an immense crowd is the capacity to contact more individuals. If you have 10,000 fans on Facebook, for instance, additional individuals will probably see your posts than if you had 1,000 fans (all else being equivalent).

Be that as it may, the size of your crowd isn't generally so significant as the relationship you work with your crowd.

It's more important to have 100 individuals on your email list that open and read each email you send them than it is to have 1,000 supporters on Twitter who seldom see your Tweets or draw in with you in any capacity.

Concerning building a group of people, faithfulness and commitment are the most significant.

Here Are The Absolute Most Familiar Ways That Web-based Course Makers Are Building Their Crowd:

1. Social Media

Set up profiles and additional pages on the informal community networks in which your interest group invests energy. You needn't bother with a presence in each virtual entertainment organization. Pick the best 2-3 that check out for yourself and center your endeavors there. Share your substance, join significant gatherings, begin your own Facebook bunch, and take part in discussions. The objective here is to construct genuine associations with others that are keen on your course subject.

2. Content Advertising

Distribute free happiness about your course subject as frequently as possible. Free satisfaction assists you with building trust and authority in your industry. Normal sorts of content that you can make are articles, recordings, digital broadcast episodes, pictures, and infographics. This assistance to build traffic to your site and openness for your business.

The more satisfied you distribute with your site and different stages (like YouTube), the more probable your interest group will find you as they are looking for data about your subject.

3. Publicity and PR

One of the speediest ways of building your crowd is to get before exiting crowds. Composing articles for well-known distributions in your industry, getting talked with on web recordings, and getting highlighted in customary media (television, radio, papers, print magazines, and so on) are extraordinary ways of expanding your openness and fabricating expertise in your industry.

4. Networking And Joint Endeavors

Construct associations with different specialists and powerhouses in your industry. It doesn't work out more or less by accident, yet constructing commonly gainful associations with others can prompt various open doors, including visitors contributing to a blog, interviews, joint endeavors, organizations, and client references.

5. Public Speaking

Connect with occasion hosts and coordinators of meetings and classes that your interest group joins in. Propose to give a show on your point. A few occasions will try to allow you to sell your course straightforwardly to their crowd, in return for a level of your deals.

A significant benefit of public talking is you stand out from everybody in the room during your show, and that can be exceptionally difficult to get on the web.

6. Email Promoting

With regards to promoting your web-based course (or any item or administration online besides), email advertising is undoubtedly the best method for producing deals. An email rundown of individuals that have communicated interest in your course subject and have allowed you to speak with them will probably be your most significant resource as a web-based course maker.

Begin fabricating your email list at the earliest opportunity. Keep in contact with your supporters by sending them supportive messages and connections to your substance consistently. This is an incredible method for procuring their trust before you request that they purchase from you.

7. Paid Promoting

Indeed, even with a humble spending plan, paid publicizing can be an incredible method for developing your crowd. By using publicizing stages like Facebook, Google, YouTube, Twitter, and LinkedIn, you can target individuals in light of explicit measures, including socioeconomics, interests, search terms, work titles, and then some. As a matter of fact, a considerable lot of Thinkific's best clients have been utilizing Facebook promotions to develop their crowd and produce predictable leads and deals for their web-based courses.

"Consistency did it for us. Accomplishing something consistently, no less than one time per week, assisted us with getting better super quick since we were investing the energy and placing in the training." - Jordan Harbinger, Creator and Web recording Host

Stage 6: Make An Internet-based Course

Making a web-based course is certainly one of the additional astonishing strides in this whole cycle, yet it can likewise be the most tedious one if you don't watch out.

A great many people spend a little while (or months, contingent upon the course) making their internet based course. Other, more experienced course makers have idealized this cycle and can make a whole web-based course at one end of the week.

In any case, paying little mind to how long it requires for you to make your course, the cycle that you go through will undoubtedly seem to be this:

1. Pick Your Course Title And Caption.
2. Guarantee That Your Point Has Appeal On The Lookout
3. Guarantee That The Learning Results Are Heavenly
4. Accumulate Material For Your Web-based Course Satisfied
5. Make An Illustration Plan (Otherwise Known As Course Frame) And Pick Your Example Types (Sound, Video, Text, And So On.)
6. Distinguish The Most Effective Ways To Convey Every One Of Your Course Modules
7. Film, Record, And Alter Your Web-based Course
8. Set Out A Plan, Including A Site
9. Pick A Cost For Your Course
10. Make A Business Page And Spotlight On Promoting Your Course

Rather than going through every one of these means in more detail here in this article (which would make it way longer than it as of now is!),

I will share a couple of the main examples we've found out about course creation from the specialists we talked with.

1. **Make A "base Practical Course"**

An idea that Eric Ries, an American essayist and business person, has promoted in his book Lean Startup: is the idea of a Base Suitable Item (BSI).

A BSI is an improvement method utilized by associations (particularly new companies) in which they create another item with adequate highlights to fulfill early adopters. The last, complete arrangement of elements is just planned and created after thinking about input from the item's underlying clients.

Applying this idea to making on the web courses, that implies that you shouldn't attempt to make the ideal course the initial time. All things considered, make a Base Suitable Course (BSC).

Here's the reason...

The issue with attempting to make the "great" course before you show it or offer it to anybody is that "awesome" is an extremely emotional term. Your thought process is amazing is most likely not equivalent to what your clients/understudies believe is awesome. Regardless of whether it is, your course doesn't need to be ideal to be significant.

Hairsplitting has prevented additional individuals from making and sending off their internet-based courses than anything more. Try not to allow this to happen to you. On the off chance that your course (defective as it could be) is adequate to help somebody, then it is sufficient to distribute. Shown improvement over great.

Make your BSC as fast as could be expected so you can distribute it and get genuine input from genuine understudies. In view of their criticism and other significant information (for example, course fruition and commitment rates) you can eliminate preparing, add preparing, and make corrections to your course to improve it.

"Try not to be a fussbudget in light of the fact that the world can hardly hang tight for great. Make it happen, get it out and get it sold. It's anything but a book, so you can continuously return to it occasionally. However, your main need is making a change in your clients, so maintain your concentration there."
- Shazzie Love, Business Strategist

2. Course Length ≠ Course Worth

One more serious mix-up to abstain from is attempting to instruct all that you are familiar to your subject in a solitary course. Doing this will doubtlessly bring about a really lengthy course that your understudies won't finish and that requires some investment to make in any case. *Wrong methodology!!*
Your web-based course is the alternative way
The reason for your course is to show your understudy how to get from Point A to Point B as fast and as effectively as could be expected. It's the alternate route.

Your web-based course is the alternative way. Assist your understudies with getting from A to B as fast as could be expected.

You totally shouldn't overpower your understudies by cerebrum unloading all that you are familiar to your point in your course. Your course ought to be essentially as short as conceivable without forfeiting the critical ideas in your preparation.

Try not to make 8 hours of preparing in the event that you can show your understudies what they need to be aware with 3 hours of preparing. However long they realize what you vowed to show them, they will not say anything negative that your course was "excessively short".

All things being equal, they'll most likely thank you for not burning through their experience with cushion or filler content.

3. Send off To A Little Experimental Group First

One more significant illustration we gained from the specialists we talked with isn't to send off the primary form of your course (your MVC!) to your whole crowd.

All things being equal, you ought to elevate your course to a little section of your crowd at a lower cost than what you in the long run need to charge for your course. Assuming you really do elevate your course to your whole crowd, consider forcing a breaking point on the quantity of understudies that can sign up for it. When you hit your objective, you briefly close enlistment for your course.

This procedure is many times called a beta send off (like pre-selling). The objective of this kind of send off is to get your course under the control of few understudies who will "test" your course. In return for getting to your course at a scaled down cost, you request that your understudies give you criticism to assist you with working on the course and tributes to use in your future showcasing.

In view of the criticism from your understudies, you can make shifts to work in your direction. At the point when you have an updated variant of your course that is superior to the first and positive understudy tributes to use in your promoting, you re-open enlistment for your course and sell it a more exorbitant cost.

Stage 7: Spotlight On Client Achievement

Alright, how about we imagine that you've proactively finished Stages 1 to 5.

1. You've concluded what theme you will instruct. It's not excessively wide, and it requests to a particular interest group.
2. You've approved market interest for your subject. Large number of individuals all over the planet are keen on it, and they're now burning through cash to learn it.
3. You've created a convincing brand. You are referred to in your industry as a specialist on your point. At the point when your dominant interest group finds you, they believe that you can help them.
4. You've fabricated a group of people. You have supporters via web-based entertainment. There are individuals on your email list.

There are different specialists in your industry that you have associations with. It has highlighted you in different distributions, webcasts, and news sources.

5. You've made a web-based course. Also, after elevating your course to your crowd, you are pleased to say that you have clients. Your business is yielding cashflow.

Although it is a tremendous achievement to get this far (and indeed, you have the right to celebrate as of now!), there is still work to be finished.

It is only the start of procuring clients. Presently, your responsibility is to follow through on the commitment you made to your clients.

Consider any neighborhood business you are a client of. A café. A nail salon. A bistro. An odds and ends shop.

These organizations don't remain in business since they are continually drawing in new clients. They stay in business because their current clients return at least a couple of times, frequently carrying their loved ones with them. This equivalent rule applies to your internet-based course business.

"We're not in this business just to get individuals to purchase our stuff. We believe that they should see the change and the effect and make the examples of overcoming adversity." - Nick Unsworth, Chief of Life on Fire

6. **Keeping A Client Than Procure Another One Is Significantly Less Expensive**

Assuming you are continually putting resources into advertising and advancement to draw in new clients, yet you're never really guaranteeing the progress of those clients, it will be truly challenging (and costly!) for you to construct a productive and maintainable business.

At the point when a client buys your web-based course, this ought not to be the conclusion of your friendship with them. This ought to be the start.

Your clients ought to be so excited with the preparation and general experience that you give to them that they buy extra courses from you later on, and they educate others regarding your courses as well.

The following are a couple of ways you can expand your understudy commitment and degrees of consistency:

1. Gamify The Opportunity For Growth

Make impetuses and offer prizes to your understudies for accomplishing explicit achievements in your course.

2. Help Your Understudies Be Responsible

Match them up with a responsibility accomplice, offer 1-on-1 or gathering training calls with your understudies, or make a confidential gathering or conversation board for them to communicate with one another.

3. Appeal To Various Learning Styles

Try not to make preparing that requests to only one learning style. Use various media types to convey your substance (text, video, sound, worksheets, tests, and so on.).

4. Create Little, Scaled Illustrations

More limited examples are bound to be finished by understudies than longer ones. If it takes you some time to show a particular idea, have a go at separating the idea into a few more limited examples.

5. Send Update Messages To Your Students

If you notice that an understudy isn't getting to or finishing the preparation in your course, send them a courteous update email to reconnect them. Show them that you give it a second thought.

Stage 8: Scale Your Business

The last move toward building an effective internet-based course business is proportional to your business by making frameworks as well as employing individuals to guarantee that it keeps on developing.

As indicated by Greg Smith, Chief of Thinkific, **you ought to just scale something that works.**

The 76 stages that preceded this one are your opportunity to do exactly that. To demonstrate that your internet-based course business works. When you have a business that works, now is the right time to move from investing most of your energy working in your business to dealing with it.

This is achieved by making frameworks and recruiting individuals to deal with the monotonous, everyday undertakings associated with maintaining your business. The objective is to let loose yourself to concentrate most of your experience on exercises that push your business ahead, for example,

1. Building your crowd
2. Building your organization
3. Making deals channels to get new clients
4. Making extra courses or potential administrations to offer to your clients

The following are a couple of the key illustrations we found out about scaling an internet-based course business from the master we talked with:

1. Mechanize Dull Errands

Recognize the errands in your business that are exceptionally monotonous and not the most ideal utilization of your experience as a businessperson. Record the interaction for those assignments and agent them to another person, or use innovation/programming to computerize that errand for you. Each dreary undertaking that you mechanize today gets you an additional opportunity to zero in on different exercises tomorrow.

"How you duplicate time is by investing energy in things today that gives you additional time tomorrow." - Rory Vaden, Southwestern Counseling

2. Build A Group As Soon As Supposed

To grow a web-based course business to 6 or even 7 figures in yearly income and then some, you will require some assistance.

Not very many business visionaries can fabricate fruitful and supportable organizations without a group of individuals to assist them with getting it going.

There is essentially a lot to learn and do, and insufficient hours in the day for one individual to do everything.

Employing a menial helper or an individual colleague is an incredible beginning stage. From that point, consider recruiting help for a different region of your business, including content creation and altering, promoting and publicizing, marking, bookkeeping, and so on. These don't need to be full-time workers.

Many course makers have groups that comprise specialists and self-employed entities from around the world.

"To go quick, go alone. If you have any desire to go the distance, go together." - African Proverbs

3. Attach Your Business To A More noteworthy Unadulterated

Sharing your insight by making the web courses is an extraordinary method for enabling others through schooling and pushing humankind ahead. In any case, making web courses is unquestionably by all accounts, not the only method for having a beneficial outcome on the planet.

There are incalculable associations that are doing extraordinary things to make the world a superior spot.

By cooperating with different associations and binding your business to a more noteworthy reason, you guarantee that as your business develops, so does the effect you make on the planet.

"Whether you're in the non-benefit structure or the for-benefit structure, you have a huge chance to involve business as a power for good." - Adam Braun, Pioneer behind Pencils of Promise

CHAPTER TWO: TESTING YOUR DEAL

WHY YOU SHOULD CONTINUOUSLY SELL BEFORE YOU MAKE

From Thought to First Client: Selling It Before You Make It

Such a long way on the excursion to your most memorable client. You've picked the crowd you'll target and taken in the issues they're willing to pay somebody to settle.

It might seem like the subsequent stage is to make your items — and it very well may be, for certain organizations. In any case, in an ideal world, you'll pre-sell your item first.

You can sell an item before you make it.

Indeed, numerous fruitful organizations were sent off along these lines.

At the point when you pre-sell your item, you offer the possibility of your answer for your crowd to check their advantage and ability to pay.

You might acknowledge cash for pre-orders as a feature of this interaction, or you may simply examine your thought with likely clients to see whether it truly addresses their issues.

Minuscule Wood Oven, an internet-based store selling little ovens for little spaces, is an incredible model. In the wake of paying attention to their crowd and recognizing an issue, they sent off a crowdfunding effort and offered pre-orders. The predominantly sure reaction affirmed that their item would be a hit and assisted transform a solitary blog with posting into a 1,000,000 dollar business.

Three Motivations To Pre-sell Your Item

1. **Line Up With Your Clients' Qualities**

You want to introduce the possibility of your item before making it. An effective pre-deal affirms that you've tracked down an important answer for a particular issue. Your objective clients will pay for it although it doesn't yet exist. That is strong.

2. **Further Develop Item Adequacy**

With some cash close by from your pre-deal, you have time and assets to improve the item. You know there's interest in this item, so it's currently worth putting resources into its turn of events.

Continuous enhancements likewise give you something to discuss with your pre-purchasers, as you share refreshes on your advancement through email or in informal communities.

3. **Limit Hazard To Your Business**

Any new business or item adventure conveys risk. With pre-deal pay close by and some affirmation that your item is attractive, you decrease your gamble.

You have cash and know how much stock you could require, which decreases your forthright expenses and assists you with settling on great monetary choices.

Envision that you attempt to pre-sell an item, taking it to many individuals in your interest group... and not a single one of them believes anything should do with it. Did you fall flat?

No! You just prevailed with regard to discovering that, assuming you put away time and cash fostering this item, barely anybody would have gotten it. So you saved time. Furthermore, you set aside cash.

Conversely, if your item pre-sells well, you have more certainty that individuals will buy and can securely put resources into promoting and item improvement.

Special Cases – *While Pre-selling Doesn't Appear To Be Needed*

There are circumstances where it doesn't appear to be legit to pre-sell. Be that as it may, even in these circumstances, you need to limit risk by being shrewd about item innovative work.

1. **Your Clients' Qualities Don't Line Up With Pre-selling**

Assuming your clients esteem expedient item conveyance - they need things now - selling them a thought and letting them know they need to hang tight for three months for a genuine item won't work.

Essentially, a few clients don't simply need it now - they need it now. If your water warmer is broken, you want it fixed, presently.

Assuming your web is down, you want it fixed, presently.

2. **You're In A Profoundly Serious Market**

In certain enterprises, there's as of now a ton of contest. Your answer might be unique, or far and away superior. In any case, on the off chance that you try out a plan to likely clients and illuminate them, it's not prepared, they may simply buy a current item.

Moreover, in this present circumstance, a pre-sell essentially isn't required. If there are now unique items taking care of a similar issue, you realize individuals will pay for an answer. Go make a decent item, and afterward market it.

Instructions To Pre-sell An Item Or Administration

There are two essential approaches to pre-sell:

> ➢ *Offer Pre-orders:* Your crowd can buy an item ahead of time and get it once it's prepared. It's really smart to offer them something in return for their understanding — a markdown, solicitations to a send-off party, or selective additional items — and to make the expected conveyance date extremely understood. Pre-orders are many times the most ideal way to

pass judgment on premium since individuals can spend their cash on your item.

> ***Sell Your Thought:*** You're not trading cash for this situation. All things being equal, the objective is to get clarification on some pressing issues and see whether it intrigued individuals. This might be the best course on the off chance that you're tweaking your thought and need more criticism before making a plunge further.

You can constantly do both! Sell your thought first and, when you know there's some interest, offer pre-orders.

Make These Moves To Effectively Pre-sell Your Item Or Administration:

1. **Create A Deal**

Begin by planning a proposition only for your crowd.

This could be unmistakable, similar to a markdown or gift if they pre-request, or immaterial, similar to a clarification of the actual item, including the advantages and highlights. Keep in mind: the objective is to see whether individuals are keen on your thought and ready to pay for it.

Then, get your proposal before your crowd. The following are a couple of ways of arriving at prospective clients:

1. **Construct A Landing Page**

A point of arrival is an independent site page made for one unambiguous reason — for this situation, introducing your proposition. It ought to be somewhat straightforward yet share data about your thought, the issue it addresses, and how it takes care of that issue. Assuming you're tolerating pre-orders, incorporate checkout usefulness and be clear about when they'll get the item. If you simply have any desire to introduce your thought and accumulate criticism, add a study.

A decent landing page has:

- ➤ **Context:** You have seconds to stand out enough to be noticed, so make your proposition quickly understood. Relate to their concern and show what your item will emphatically mean for their life.
- ➤ **Credibility:** Your crowd needs to trust you to follow through on your thought (or genuinely convey a pre-requested item). This could mean including certifications or experience, or simply making a presentation page that heaps rapidly, is secure, and looks proficient.
- ➤ *A Summon to Action:* On the off chance that you're accepting pre-orders, utilize an immediate expression like "Request Now." Assuming that you're searching for input, use something like "Offer Your Considerations."

Whenever you've made a presentation page, help it before your crowd through web-based entertainment, computerized promotions, or email showcasing.

2. Make A Crowdfunding Effort

Crowdfunding sites, such as Kickstarter and Indiegogo, interface your business to individuals who might be keen on your thought.

Make a profile for your thought or item, exhibit why it's helpful, and let individuals promise cash in return for the completed variant not too far off. You can put forth a raising support objective, and on the off chance that you don't arrive at it,

Everybody gets their cash back with no damage done. You don't risk making the item before you've demonstrated interest and benefactors don't risk adding to something that won't ever occur. Individuals who contribute on Kickstarter comprehend that they will not get the item immediately. They're glad to be a piece of making something that will help them and will pay ahead of time to be one of the first to get it.

3. Contact Your Crowd Where They Assemble

Associate with your crowd where they as of now invest energy. Go to a celebration, career expo, or occasion where you can converse with individuals one on one. Join Facebook bunches with themes connected with your thought. Pose inquiries on Reddit. If you, as of now, have a laid-out virtual entertainment following or email list, open it up for conversation.

Present your thought in a survey or overview, or pose open inquiries like:
- Is this item something you'd be keen on?
- How might you utilize this item?
- Might you want to pay for this item and, provided that this is true, how much?

2. Test The Deal

Whenever you've made your deal, now is the ideal time to perceive how individuals answer! Did many individuals visit your greeting page, yet entirely a couple bought? Are individuals amped up for your thought and able to purchase not too far off? Did you get any thoughts regarding how your item could be far superior? The main thing here is to be receptive.

Answer the criticism you gather and be prepared to change your thought depending on the situation.

3. Repeat As Needed

If the criticism was positive and your crowd was energized, you're great to move to the subsequent stage! Assuming you changed your thought or even exchanged arrangements completely, go through the cycle once more. Contact those individuals and check whether your progressions better fit their necessities.

4. Confirm Your Worth

Pre-offering allows you an opportunity to zero in on taking care of an issue for your ideal interest group and affirms the worth of your answer. Make a move to sell them on the thought so you can consummate your item and convey it by your assessed date.

Presently, it is the right time to make items for your energized clients!

Elements To Think About Before You Sell

Online deals can expand your market and increment income for your business. However, several variables ought to be thought about. Except if drew nearer accurately, you risk discoloring the standing of your organization if you can't follow through on what is guaranteed. Because of the planned operations engaged with getting the item into your clients' hands, losing cash on the venture is additionally conceivable. Furthermore, because selling on the web implies you're rivaling every seller in your market, you likewise need to zero in on showcasing.

There are various variables to consider before offering to guarantee a positive outcome:

1. **Rivalry**

All organizations face contests, and achievement is much of the time because of how well you answer it. You ought to know about your rivals and consistently endeavor to foster an upper hand over them.

To acquire an upper hand, you could:
- ➤ *Raise Or Lower Your Costs.*
- ➤ *Improve Your Item Or Administration* - improving or modernizing highlights or the assembling system
- ➤ *Use Inventive Channels Of Conveyance* - for example, channels of appropriation not typically connected with your item or administration.

2. **Take Advantage Of Provider Connections**

Before spreading out to online businesses, it is vital to figure out what sort of rivalry you will confront. If you are selling something promptly accessible from other web-based retailers, you could battle to acquire traction except if you can offer more cutthroat costs. Individuals are bound to buy from a laid-out retailer that they have managed before, when the cost distinction for items is insignificant. Contenders could likewise have arrangements and advancements setup that you can't coordinate. Concentrating on the opposition likewise permits you to see what they are doing well and how you might improve while wandering into online deals.

3. **The Portion Of The Overall Industry**

A piece of the pie is the level of all deals inside a market that is held by one brand/item or organization and can be estimated in more ways than one. For example:
- Deals Income
- Deals Volume

A portion of the overall industry is straightforwardly connected with productivity and many organizations intend to build their business comparative with their rivals.

You can quantify your organization's presentation comparative with a contender by the extent of the market that your organization can catch - Piece of the pie = organization deals isolated by complete market deals.

You can increase the piece of the pie by:
- ***Offering More Benefits For Expected Clients*** - for example, further developing item quality.
- ***Cost Cutting*** - to increment deals' income. However, this strategy may not succeed if contenders are willing and ready to meet any cost cuts.
- ***Adding New Channels Of Dissemination Or Expanding The Force Of Laid-out Dispersion Channels.***

> *Advancement* - expanding promotion use, however, contenders might answer as needs be.

4. **Client Base**

The purchasers that purchase your business' labor and products characterize your client base. Consider the things you ought to be familiar with them, including why they could purchase from you.

5. **Specialties**

A specialty is a little yet productive segment of a market that is frequently reasonable for a particular scope of labor and products that meet a specific need. You can make a specialty market by recognizing client needs or needs that are not being addressed by contenders and by offering items to those clients.

6. **Showcasing System**

Your organization will require an advanced showcasing system that will go about as your promoting guide and structure a fundamental piece of your general marketable strategy.

7. **Brand Message**

Before you start to sell an item or administration, you ought to pose one inquiry of your organization - what does your image rely on?

For your image to hang out in the commercial center, it ought to make a close-to-home association with expected clients.

You ought to intend to sell an encounter as opposed to an item, for instance, a monetary help to give inner serenity.

8. **Discount Esteem**

A few items are sold through wholesalers. Wholesalers purchase products from makers at a marked-down cost. In the wake of adding to their net revenue, they then supply the merchandise to retailers who offer it to the general population.

Most organizations will want to offer to wholesalers, as they can give an effective method for arriving at numerous retailers on the double. Be that as it may, you ought to take a gander at the net revenue you want to make to stay productive. This is vital to guarantee you don't sell your items too efficiently to the distributor who will constantly need the most minimal conceivable cost from their providers.

9. **Coordinated Operations Of Conveying The Item**

Another component you ought to think about is the coordinated operations of getting it done for the client. On the off chance that you are selling a computerized item, you should have the framework set up to permit clients to download it easily. If you can't dispense adequate data transmission, you'll experience a ton of issues if the request surpasses your assumptions, for example, slow download paces or server mistakes while endeavoring to employ your administration. For actual items, you want to investigate the operations of delivery and protection which could eat into your benefits except if thought about it

10. **Security**

Security is a major issue for the two purchasers and merchants online. Online organizations are rewarding focuses for programmers searching for client data and records. It's your obligation to shield your clients' data, as a security break won't just be extremely badly designed for your clients, but will likewise make seriously harm your standing. Ensure you have powerful techniques set up to forestall any possibility of misusing client data.

11. **Internet Promoting**

Showcasing your item online requires openness via virtual entertainment destinations, as well as designated promotions intended to direct people to your webpage.

You will likewise have to make or refresh your organization site so it is not difficult to explore and is interesting to guests. An inadequately planned site will disappoint guests and could dissuade them from utilizing your administration.

Ensure that your site will want to deal with the convergence of guests as the people who can't get to your sight probably won't try to return to it later.

12. Deals Advancement Models

You can utilize advancement to empower deals of your item or administration. Deals advancements are much of the time unique and innovative and there are numerous famous choices, for instance:

1. *Get One-Get-One-Free*
1. *Motivating Forces, For Example, Extra Tips, Vouchers, Cash-off Coupons, Rivalries, And Prize Draws*
2. *Time-delicate Motivations Can Be Utilized To Urge Clients To Purchase Immediately*
3. *Retail Location Materials And Item Shows.*
4. *Unconditional Gifts And Loyalty Tips*
5. *Limited Costs.*
6. *Joint Advancements – Between Brands Claimed By A Similar Organization Or With A Brand From Another Organization.*
7. *Free Samples.*
8. *Fair-exchange And Cause-related Items, For Example, Those Which Help A Good Cause.*
9. *Finance Bargains – No Or Low Money Or Purchase Presently Pay Later.*
10. *Unique Arrangements For Initial-time Clients To Divert Them From Programs Into Buyers.*
11. *Online Coupons For Clients Who Have Enlisted For A Record Or Bought Into A Bulletin.*

It is essential to guarantee that any advancements and offers will notwithstanding make you a benefit regardless of whether extremely fruitful and taken up by loads of clients.

13. Bargaining

Decisively, bargaining is vital as it is essential for item situating. It influences other
showcasing components, for example, item elements, appropriation, and advancement.

There are numerous ways to bargain for an item, for instance :

- ***Premium Bargain*** - an exorbitant cost for exceptional items or administrations
- ***Entrance Bargain*** - a falsely low cost to acquire a portion of the overall industry before expanding the cost
- ***Economy Bargain*** - straightforward low cost normally connected with economy brands
- ***Promotional Bargain***

14. Web-based Selling

To sell online effectively, the standards of customary selling apply. You should have an item or administration that potential clients need, at a value they can bear from which you can create a gain. The last step is to ensure your potential clients are familiar with your item or administration.

15. Online Shop

You want to make it as simple as workable for expected clients to think that you are on the web and purchase from you. You want to give all the data that clients expect to settle on a choice and simplify it to finish the cycle. Consider things that could be a hindrance to clients finishing the deal, for example, befuddling route or surprising conveyance costs.

To amplify deals,
1. Ensure your site is not difficult to track down, alluring, and easy to comprehend and utilize.

2. Concentrate on best practices in website composition while making your site.
3. Use website streamlining (Web optimization) to make your website simple to track down through web search tools.
4. Make an internet-based shop for more information on fostering an internet business webpage.

16. Showcasing On The Web

To showcase your item or administration online, you want to consider how potential clients will track down your site, for instance, through a web search tool.

17. Laying Out Your Deals Targets

Guide:

To effectively put up another item or administration for sale to the public, you should follow a few fundamental stages:

1. *Con The Market*

You ought to concentrate on your rivals' promoting materials (adverts, sites, and so on) and distinguish where your item or administration is comparable and where it isn't. You can then survey if clients are probably going to purchase from your or your rivals.

This data will likewise uncover the ideal client for your item or administration that you can then focus on with your advertising.

A decent strategy to utilize is a SWOT (Strengths, Weaknesses, Opportunity, and Threats) examination.

2. *Characterize Your Advertising Strategy And Techniques*

You should pick the right deals and advertising channels for your item/administration, for example, shop, site, or both.

Generally, a business that sells across many channels will make more noteworthy progress since clients who can shop when and any way they like will more often than not spend more and shop on a more regular basis.

You ought to ensure that whatever number of individuals could be allowed to have some familiarity with your item or administration, including expected clients, the media, and commentators.

In the wake of presenting your item or administration, it should refresh your promoting effort as your item or administration develops.

Via cautiously checking your advertising results, you will want to see unavoidable losses that will demonstrate when the time has come to:

> *Reexamine the item or administration*
> *Change your media message*
> *Get rid of and send off another item/administration.*

3. Create Your Deals Plan

In a business both on the web and disconnected, your definitive objective is to bring in cash. To assist you with doing this a deals plan is required.

A deals plan depicts and evaluates throughout some period how deals of your items or administrations will be made and to whom.

A deals plan incorporates data about your business and clients. It can assist you with outlining ways of expanding deals with current clients as well as extending your business to draw in new clients.

A fruitful deals plan is noteworthy and has a technique for assessing results once the arrangement has run its course.

You would typically make your own deals plan, frequently with the contribution of representatives and so forth.

WHAT ISSUES COULD SEEM WHILE SETTING UP A BUSINESS ON THE WEB?

Beginning a business online is quicker, simpler, and more reasonable than any other time in recent memory, yet it's not without its traps. Specialized issues, security issues, and shopper doubt are every one of the pieces of maintaining a business on the web. While you can forestall or if nothing else manage these issues, entrepreneurs should continually screen likely issues to stay away from serious fiascos.

1. **Specialized Issues**

Specialized issues are genuinely normal in web-based business fire up.
There could be a similarity issue in which the webpage proprietor is attempting
to run content - coded guidelines that the site executes, like a structure accommodation - or a program that won't work with the host supplier's servers. Or differently, there can be an issue in the coding of the site or the programming of content. The more educated the website proprietor and his website admin are tied in with coding and programming, the simpler it is to find and fix these issues.

2. **Server Unwavering Quality**

Sadly, no web has can offer 100% up time— the period during which the webpage is running. Eventually, all servers crash and your site will go down with it. That may be the site's issue, either due to an excess of traffic or transfer speed use, or content the site could do without. It additionally could be the web host's concern. The most ideal way to manage this issue is to every so often back up your site to your nearby PC or outsider stockpiling and pick a web to have with high up-time unwavering quality.

3. **Security**

Security breaches can cut your webpage down, ruin your web-based standing and undermine your clients' protected data. Safeguarding that data, particularly about installments, is critical to maintaining an effective internet-based business.

Online destinations that take installments need to have secure attachment layers-- electronic conventions for overseeing security when shoppers submit data on the web. You'll likewise need to utilize secure installment-handling frameworks. Utilize a novel, undecipherable login, and passwords to get to managerial segments of your site to forestall hacking.

 4. **Unfortunate Promotion**

Advertising is vital for online business achievement. Tragically, numerous internet-based entrepreneurs don't have a very arranged or executed showcasing plan. Online entrepreneurs can't depend on web crawlers alone to send clients, and on second thought, ought to have a progression of promoting methodologies, for example, publicizing, official statements, articles, and person-to-person communication. The site needs to impart client certainty by having contact data, protection and security data, and quality client assistance.

WHAT TO SELL ON THE WEB: HOW TO TRACK DOWN ITEMS TO OUTSOURCE

Ok, the ageless inquiry of the new web-based business person.

You need to find items that are famous and make you a delightful benefit. Yet, how in the world do you pick what to sell on the web?

One of the most incredible methodologies is to jump straight into the information readily available. Find high-likely items by diving profound into some run-of-the-mill item research.

Uncertain How To Explore This?

You're perfectly positioned. The article will give you a guide for thinking of the best outsourcing item thoughts and give you the information to decisively sift through the ones which do not merit testing.

Regardless if you're an internet business startup or a laid-out little or medium-sized business, you'll track down a lot of supportive information to get a scrumptious lift in your net revenues.

Why Sell Items Online With Outsourcing?
Before we dig into sorting out what to sell on the web, I need to offer a speedy clarification of what outsourcing is and the advantages of settling on this plan of action.
Along these lines, you'll have a superior comprehension of the one-of-a-kind contemplations that you want to effectively track down which things to sell on the web.

All In All, What Is Outsourcing?
Outsourcing is an undeniably well-known type of web-based business where vendors import items from outsider providers and sell them in their web-based stores. Along these lines, they can reduce the expenses and liabilities of loading stock themselves.

Dropshippers can choose their cost markups and can maintain their organizations from practically any place on the planet.

Outsourcing likewise allows web-based business visionaries to keep steady over the latest things since they can undoubtedly change the product sold in their stores at whatever point they need.

These are only a couple of the advantages of picking outsourcing over additional customary assortments of web-based business. Everything necessary to create some serious benefit is tracking down the right items to offer to the perfect market at the ideal time.

Presently, how about we investigate the absolute prescribed procedures for concocting winning outsourcing item thoughts?

What To Sell On The Web: How To Track Down Items To Outsource?

1. Conceptualize Outsourcing Item Thoughts

You never need to begin a clear page. Your head is now loaded with the best things to outsource: your side interests, items you like, and newfound interests.

Utilizing instruments like Google Patterns can uncover additional opportunities and excuse item speculations so you can design your outsourcing business.

effectively. Begin by taking advantage of the abundance of data and motivation you as of now have drifted around in your mind.

Record all that rings a bell. It doesn't make any difference if you figure the item will be a hit or not. Try not to avoid this step, as it gives a significant establishment to the following ones.

Track Down Items To Sell Online Through Perusing Different Shops

Harking back to the 1980s, Walmart's organizer Sam Walton was captured for slithering around stores on all fours. He later told a companion he was estimating the spaces between item retires to decide how his rivals showed their items.

At that point, Walmart was making $400M+ in deals, however, Walton realize that there was more he could procure - if by some stroke of good luck he could dominate the methodologies his rivals were utilizing to sell their items.

At the point when you peruse different stores, take a gander at their contributions, top-rated records, and advanced items.

Many stores have a huge measure of information and utilize entire divisions to coordinate their deals and select their items. Utilize that data to your advantage. Peruse a ton and peruse as often as possible. It'll assist you with finding the ideal outsourcing items to sell online through your retail facade.

Here is a rundown of stores and assets you ought to take a gander at consistently:

- *Amazon Best Sellers*
- *eBay Everyday Deals*

- *LightInTheBox Top Dealers List*
- *Our What to Sell On the web*

At the point when you track down any outsourcing thoughts that arouse your curiosity, add them to your item list.

2. Find The Best Outsourcing Items On Friendly Shopping Destinations

There are lord lots of 100 million items on Polyvore and 30 million on Wanelo. Add Extravagant, Pinterest, and even Instagram to the blend, and you have countless items from around the world. Moreover, they can undoubtedly be arranged by ubiquity, patterns, and classifications, and that's only the tip of the iceberg.

Individuals frequently ignore these destinations in their examination, however, they're significant for drawing experiences about which sorts of items are causing disturbances on the web over time.

I suggest setting up a record on every single one of these sites. Buy into various classifications and records. Follow what individuals like the most and add those things to your rundown.

At the point when you're continually encircling yourself with motivation, you'll immediately concoct item thoughts that have benefit-creating potential.

Ask Your Companions For Outsourcing Thoughts

The following time you have espresso with companions, research some Google Patterns information on famous items in advance and get some information about those things.

Try not to restrict yourself to your socioeconomics, all things considered. Converse with companions of any age and foundation to get a wide assortment of outsourcing thoughts and a more extensive scope of viewpoints about what stuff to sell on the web.

You'll probably wind up with outsourcing thoughts you hadn't even thought of, and these will make your online business store greatly improved.

3. ***Check Out You For Extra Thoughts Regarding What To Sell On The Web***

Check out your home, your work area, and the spots locally that you as often as possible visit.

Are there any items you can't survive without? Which items could make your life more straightforward? Is there whatever's difficult to come by in the general store or at neighborhood shops?

The responses to these inquiries could hold the key while you're choosing what to sell online by employing your store.

Think about this: Howard Schultz concocted his bistro, thought out traveling to Italy and later called it Starbucks.

Bunches of outsourcing item thoughts can ring a bell while voyaging, yet spotting them locally in regular day-to-day existence is comparably conceivable. Begin involving your everyday existence similar to claim databank for item thoughts. Remain alarmed and spot open doors.

When you take on this mentality, you'll begin to see many items with significant benefits expected every day.

While you're being dynamic with your ideation, you'll immediately think of a rundown of the best outsourcing items for your store. Thus, be perceptive, convey a scratch pad, and make sure to put everything on paper.

Destinations To Keep Away From While Thinking Of Outsourcing Thoughts

While thinking of your rundown of items to sell on the web, I recommend you don't see destinations like SpringWise.com or TrendHunter.com.
It isn't so much that they're intrinsically awful. They're perfect for different purposes, truth be told.

Yet, with regards to creating item thoughts and choosing what things to sell, item pattern locales distribute thoughts that are much of the time far off for the typical dealer. That is because there is much of the time an excessive number of other people who have proactively gotten on board with that fleeting trend of selling these things.

In different cases, these items are too challenging to even think about getting for outsourcing. So while you could get great outsourcing item thoughts, you're probably going to battle with tracking down providers for those things.

For instance, how might you import and advance Wearable Sleeves that Assist with stroking Casualties Recuperate or Spice Motivated Aromas with outsourcing?

WHAT TO SELL ON THE INTERNET: SETTLING ON TOP-SELLING ITEMS

Then we'll cover how to limit your outsourcing item thoughts list by separating them under the accompanying contemplations. Along these lines, you should be rest assured that your rundown just has the absolute best outsourcing items.

Note that your outsourcing thoughts rundown will progress as you keep on drawing motivation and finding new item drifts.

Anybody can bring many well-known items into their stores in only a couple of moments.

The interesting part is knowing how to sort out what things to sell online because of what will likewise fit with your promoting efforts, show well on your landing page, and by and large appear to be legit inside the setting of your image.

These sorts of top-selling items are called 'Alpha Items.' They're things that attract loads of traffic to your store. After you've tracked down your Alpha Items, it's a breeze to fill in the remainder of the store by strategically pitching, upselling and related items.

1. Figure Out The Specialty To Track Down Outsourcing Item Thoughts

With the ascent of outsourcing, specialty shops have turned into a pattern. Specialties have since abandoned an online business curiosity about a demonstrated, fruitful procedure.

It appears to be legit. There's no utilization in battling with the enormous stores for potential clients' consideration.

Stay away from classifications that are excessively expansive or general. The majority are as of now presented with many offers day to day.

All things considered, hope to supply specialty items that are underserved by the bigger players. For instance, there's no particular vested party for a typical belt, however, you can undoubtedly tell that cycling stuff will resound well with cycling fans.

Find your specialty market. On the off chance that you can concoct specialty outsourcing item thoughts or even one-item store thoughts, you're now bound to make money when you sell items on the web. Get going by selling items from a consistent outsourcing specialty, since those things are probably going to be popular.

2. The 'Stay Away' Classifications While Tracking Down Items To Sell On The Web

Regardless of whether a portion of the items in this classification might cover with specialty items, it's fundamental to restrict your item choice by barring things recorded in the 'stay away' classifications.

Some item classifications have developed essentially over the course of the past ten years, and there are as of now such numerous areas of strength for more modest shops out there providing these things.

Simply check out the top internet shopping classes: furniture and apparatuses unquestionably aren't taking care of business. In the interim, buyers have spent over 759 billion on design-related things, and that implies they as of now have their decision of confidence coming up.

Cross off the accompanying general classes from your thought list: books, apparatuses, regular items, and sports. You'll have to stay away from item-related outsourcing botches if you have any desire to find success. You'll likewise be more unambiguous by tracking down a specialty.

Kindly note: I don't recommend crossing out these classes completely. You could sell modified books, custom climbing/cycling hardware gear, or a touchless cleanser allocator.

Nonetheless, I recommend you focus harder on finding a fascinating subcategory that will make your store remarkable. Try not to fall into the snare of selling things in everyday classifications.

3. Distinguish Online Items That Clients Will Purchase More Than Once

Now and again, one-off web-based orders are outstanding, however assuming that you're picking items with little net revenue, depending on many individuals, purchasing your item once isn't the most ideal methodology for life span.

Consider online items that individuals will more than once purchase from you after some time and assemble brand unwavering with them. Beauty care products, apparel, and party supplies are instances of items that individuals will require ordinarily during the year.

Focusing on them with remarketing efforts after their most memorable buy, and circling back to customized email showcasing, you will make an extraordinary relationship that will lead them back to you later on.

The lifetime worth of these clients can be higher than all your oddball clients assuming you plan your repair mission to suit them.

4. Take A Look At Interest Through Virtual Entertainment

Virtual entertainment is an incredible spot to search for proof of client interest. Looking for the name of your picked item on YouTube is an incredible method for seeing if individuals are doing unpacking surveys or turning into web sensations with video tributes.

You can likewise look at the remarks on recordings to check whether there are any issues with the item you should know about.

Remember, other virtual entertainment channels like Facebook and Instagram. You can utilize Facebook search to look at which recordings are becoming famous online in your industry, or for a specific catchphrase. You'll likewise have the option to redo your hunt to find out where certain words are moving most.

Instagram likewise gives you an astounding method for investigating items. You should simply search for terms pertinent to your industry in the hunt bar. Look at items that are certainly standing out from individuals in your space.

Simply be mindful to guarantee that items aren't moving via virtual entertainment for some unacceptable reasons. Recordings can become a web sensation on YouTube when individuals love an item, yet individuals likewise utilize virtual entertainment to whine about things they hate. Look into the item before you contribute and ensure the consideration is positive.

5. Utilize The Cost Perfect Balance

There are a couple of overall principles to recollect while considering what to sell on the web: the lower the value, the better the transformation rate. The higher the value, the more exertion you'll have to make.

Andrew from ecommerceFuel says the ideal web-based business item cost range is from $100 to $200. Richard from ABLS contends that it's $75 to $150. As far as I can tell, my perfect balance cost is $40 to $60 (at a 200% markup).

Inside the $40 to $60 cost range, the benefits are sufficiently high that you can, in any case, cover your promoting and transporting expenses of up to $20 per deal. The transformation rate is generally higher inside this cost range than a pricier section because the buy requires less thought for the purchaser. You regularly will not bring to the table as much client service with more affordable things.

Hence alone, you increment the chances of the progress of your store in creating markets. With Chinese outsourcing, you can sell stuff wherever on the planet. Although you need to remember that while $30 may not be a lot to individuals living in the US, it very well may be a great deal for somebody in South America or Eastern/Focal Europe.

Reward Secret: You ought to take a stab at selling stuff in creating or dismissing markets. Lower promoting expenses and contest rise to a higher return for capital invested. Try not to stress over the language boundary.

In this manner, it's consistently advantageous to explore various business sectors while choosing where to sell your items. As of now, I recommend investigating your rundown and crossing out any outsourcing thoughts that are more than $60.

6. Leverage ePacket For Your Outsourcing Items

ePacket is an incredible help that considers quick transportation from China to more than 30 nations across the world. Simply make certain to chase after every one of the standards of weight and size. An item's weight can't be multiple kgs. The bundle size should be somewhere around 14 cm x 11 cm, and something like 90 cm between the length, width, and level. Also, the worth of the item being delivered can't be more than $400.

7. Pick An Outsourcing Item That Endures

Remember that the outsourcing items you sell online can be sent to any area of the planet except if you set a few boundaries. This implies that conveyance could be a long cycle, including a ton of dumping and reloading.

Assuming you pick delicate items, similar to china adornments, they might get broken on the way. This is the kind of thing you don't have to command over. What's more, it can prompt miserable clients and many returns, which can hurt your store's believability.

The focal point? Pick an item that is powerful and can endure long travel times to save yourself time on discounts and returns. These things eat into your business benefits.

8. Sort Through Surveys To Approve Items

Surveys aren't simply a decent wellspring of experiences for different shoppers. They're likewise a phenomenal method for concluding whether an item has an incentive for your image.

If you, as of now, have a store, figure out what individuals are talking about your current items. Perhaps you'll find input and remarks that assist you with sorting out what you ought to sell straightaway. For example, perhaps your client adores your attire item but wants to offer more sizes or varieties.

If you don't have a store, look at surveys for items in the business you like. Figure out which items are moving with devices like Google Patterns, and ask yourself what clients like and abhorrence about every item.

While you'll presumably avoid items with a lot of negative surveys, a couple of terrible audits could likewise be a decent sign. Assuming your clients love the item but disdain the bundling or conveyance administration, you have a quick method for separating your image by taking care of those issues.

9. Realize Your Promoting Channels To Sell Additional Outsourcing Items

After you figure out how to sell items online that can create a decent gain, you need to ponder your promoting procedure. Having great outsourcing item thoughts isn't sufficient.

You should have an arrangement for how you'll sell these items. This is a significant piece of finding success in the web-based business.

If you have the right promoting plan, you can sell stuff online all the more without any problem. Promoting is the essential way you'll stand apart from your rivals, and being known all about the different showcasing channels available to you will be priceless to your business.

To lay it out plainly, unique promoting channels will be more famous for various items. When you pick the item, you need to sort out which advertising channel will be best for it. Explore different avenues regarding free promoting channels to get a vibe of how the crowd could respond when they see your items, and afterward, take it from that point.

Promoting an $800 hoverboard on Facebook probably won't be the smartest thought, yet you could prevail with regards to publicizing it on Google Advertisements. A hoverboard is certainly not an unconstrained buy, and much of the time, individuals will research it to learn more data about it, including which stores are selling it.

I've gone through numerous hours taking a gander at how others pick their promoting procedures and found nothing that would address my issues. I preferred Rand from Moz's tables addressing the return on initial capital investment, exertion, and cost of each showcasing channel, yet it is by all accounts obsolete (distributed in 2009).

There are likewise a lot of express aides and arrangements of all promoting channels, yet not even one of them position showcasing from a stock viewpoint. Thus, I chose to do an item assessment and showcase the table myself. Its plan is like the one from Moz's blog, however, because of individual experience alongside certain considerations and bits of knowledge I've consolidated from the web.

There are many other showcasing channels out there, however, I question that PR stunts, co-marking open doors, or video advertising will be the best choices for anybody simply beginning their business.

In any case, you should consider subsidiary showcasing later on, so it's something worth talking about remembering. Make sure to inspect your assets (time, cash, information), and afterward pick a couple of showcasing channels that are possible for your conditions. Then, at that point, cross out all outsourcing thoughts that sometimes fall short for those channels.

10. Catchphrase Instruments And Google Patterns

Watchword devices and Google Patterns are an unquestionable requirement if you will involve Google Promotions as a showcasing channel or on the other hand on the off chance that you're simply commonly attempting to help natural traffic to your site.

These assist you with seeing which items are as of now moving. You can likewise actually look at the interest for your outsourcing item thoughts with these devices.

Catchphrase Device

Investigate your item thoughts. Enter every item name and variety into the Google Catchphrase Organizer device. The framework will then, at that point, create information about how cutthroat the catchphrases are, which will provide you with some sign of how much rivalry you may be facing in endeavoring to sell those items in your store.

The more cutthroat the catchphrase, the pricier it will be to utilize it on Google Advertisements.

Select 'Watchwords Thoughts,' and take a gander at the number of searches each Low Rivalry Catchphrase gets. While beginning, it's great to focus on these watchwords since they'll be more financially plan well disposed, and you'll be facing less contest when an individual looks for that item on Google. Suppose you could get the entirety of that traffic and 2% of them would purchase at your store. Could this request be sufficient? The key is to figure out a perfect balance between sufficient interest and enough contest so that your items will stand apart from the group.

Note: *Other than Google's watchword programming, you can utilize these 18 Web optimization instruments to do your examination. Some of them require a month-to-month membership, however, they're significantly more remarkable when creating information about the catchphrase contest.*

Google Patterns

Go to trends.google.com and do a similar activity here. Enter every one of your item thoughts into the inquiry and decide the patterns of interest in light of search volume. Besides the fact that you have can a gander at what's as of now moving, however, you can likewise see information about the recurrence of a given catchphrase search after some time.

Is the pattern expanding or diminishing? Are there any examples? Do you see any spikes? This data can be exceptionally helpful in concluding whether it's the ideal opportunity to sell a given item. Google Patterns can likewise assist you with having a more clear comprehension of client conduct, as you can see search information because of things like nation or locale.

11. Step-by-step Instructions To Know Which Items To Sell On The Web

By and large, items to stay away from outsourcing incorporate classes that have next-to-zero pursuit traffic (under 500 month-to-month looks).

Assuming you're intending to develop naturally, you ought to likewise fix all item thoughts that have a high rivalry as indicated by the Google Watchword Investigation Instrument.

You need to find the right harmony between a hunt volume that is not excessively serious, yet is sufficiently still to show that there's an interest in that item. Everything without question revolves around balance.

12. Using Irregularity To Figure Out What To Sell On The Web

While it could be energizing to see that there's a spike in interest for an item in Google, watch out. It may be the case that the item is popular because of the season.

For instance, keep away from occasional items like Christmas beautifications (except if you intend to shut everything down after special times of the year). By concentrating on occasional things, you're diminishing your deals cycle.

Most Christmas improvement deals happen in harvest time and winter. These are reasonably the absolute best outsourcing thoughts for this season. However, to endure, you'll require center items in your store that will sell the entire year.

Selling stuff online isn't simple when things are impacted via irregularity. Have an all the more long-haul technique by deciding to sell a blended match of things online that are famous in various seasons.

Practice Watchfulness With Protected Pictures

Be cautious while you're obtaining marked things for your store. It is generally difficult to distinguish providers that sell protected items.

If you're obtaining protected items from generally secret providers, quite possibly you'll sell counterfeit things. Things with logos and plans that are something similar or even excessively like different brands can prompt legitimate issues or at any rate, discolor the standing of your business.

That is the reason you can never be too wary while picking things on these grounds. We recommend avoiding anything looking like a current brand and spotlight on building your image all things being equal. This is more reasonable over the long haul. Furthermore, you'll grow a business you can be pleased with.

13. Rivalry Contemplations For What Stuff To Sell On The Web

As of now, you've had the option to refine your rundown in light of demonstrated procedures for doing as such, and you're left with the last outsourcing thoughts.

The last significant thought is a rivalry. By crossing out the general classifications we discussed above, you've previously stayed away from the contest against monster retailers like Amazon.

In any case, don't believe you're the only one out there who thought of selling specialty items. Assessing your opposition is an interminable undertaking, and there are countless ways of getting it done. However, one thing is sure. You want to check whether the item you're going to promote is now inescapable on different sites.

Here is a straightforward stunt:

Google an item, then take a stab at doing an item picture search. Take a gander at the number of shops that have comparable things available to be purchased. Assuming you're outsourcing, most storekeepers will probably have similar pictures. Track down your rivals. Then, at that point, actually take a look at their valuing procedure, notoriety and traffic (on destinations like Alexa.org or SpyFu.com), and which promoting channels they're utilizing. Cross out all item thoughts that as of now have a gigantic rivalry.

14. Request Tests From Providers

Whenever you've picked some outsourcing items to sell on your internet-based store, go ahead and demand a few examples from the providers and make a halfhearted effort that your clients will go through.

Find out about conveyance times, item quality, and abilities to follow so you can remain by your contribution.

Go Forward and Sell Amazing Stuff

As an online business person, you want an unmistakable item determination process set up to sort out which things truly have benefit potential for your business.

Individuals frequently pick outsourcing item thoughts spontaneously, as opposed to through cautious thought. Unfortunately, this burns through a ton of time and exertion.

Utilize the contemplations spread around here to limit your rundown and sort out what items to sell. Get some margin to dive into research so you can track down the best outsourcing item thoughts for your online business store.

In an outline, here are the contemplations to make while choosing what to sell on the web:

1. *Supply specialty items that are underserved by the bigger market.*
2. *Avoid general things that don't have an immense interest.*
3. *Recognize online items that clients will purchase over and over.*
4. *Approve requests through web-based entertainment research.*
5. *Set a cost range that persuades purchasers to buy.*
6. *Influence ePacket for your items.*
7. *Pick an outsourcing item that endures.*
8. *Sort through audits to approve items.*
9. *Realize your advertising channels to sell more things.*
10. *Leverage catchphrase instruments and Google Patterns.*

11. Track down a harmony between the interest and intensity of an item.
12. Use irregularity to figure out what to sell on the web.
13. Take a look at contender sites to distinguish immersed item thoughts.
14. Request tests from providers to find out about conveyance times.

Finally, recollect that you're continuously advancing as you go. You'll have to test your thoughts - and don't be frustrated assuming you want to attempt different thoughts before you make progress. That is the situation about beginning a business.

WHAT TO SELL ON THE WEB: WHERE TO SELL THINGS ON THE WEB

Whenever you've settled on your rundown of outsourcing items, now is the ideal time to pick where to sell these things on the web.

Will you have a site? Will you sell things over virtual entertainment? Could you at any point work with powerhouses to fabricate a brand that everybody needs?

These are significant inquiries to pose before you move to the following period of your online business venture. Do an inside-and-out contender investigation of purchasing patterns so you can see what your opposition is doing and where they're selling their items on the web. This will provide you with a smart thought of where to begin.

1. Setting Up Your Site

Selling items online is customarily finished through a site. To have one, you want to pick a web-based business site stage to have it on, such as Shopify.

If you need to outsource through Shopify, you can utilize an application like DSers to kick yourself off.

Whenever you've joined, you can pick your site format and begin to design the pages and content that should be on your site. Then, you want to import your items utilizing the DSers application to your Shopify store. Make a point to create tempting item depictions that your clients will cherish.

Before you push your site live, you'll have to test your checkout cycle to ensure that everything moves along as expected and the means are properly aligned. What's more, in the final lap, you'll pick another area for your web-based store.

2. Selling On Facebook

If your crowd is dynamic on Facebook, why not make it simple for your items to be found? You can do this by setting up a Facebook Shop.

The following are seven speedy moves toward getting this going:

Stage 1: *Interface Your Shopify Store To Your Facebook Page*

Stage 2: *Pick Which Items And Assortments To Show On Facebook*

Stage 3: *Add The "shop" Tab To Your Facebook Business Page*

Stage 4: *Arrange Your Facebook Shop Tab Inside Shopify*

Stage 5: *Add Items To Your Facebook Shop*

Stage 6: *Label Items In Facebook Posts*

Stage 7: *Deal With Your Items And Orders*

Presto. You can begin to sell on Facebook and burn through a touch of cash on promotion.

3. Selling On Instagram

Before you choose if you have any desire to sell your items on Instagram, check to assume that your nation is qualified for this element. Assuming that it is, you can fire setting up your Instagram Shop for business.

Here are the moves toward taking with a Shopify store:

Stage 1: *Associate Your Instagram Account With Your Facebook Business Page*

Stage 2: *Set Up An Instagram Business Account*

Stage 3: *Introduce Instagram Deals Directly In Shopify*

Stage 4: *Transfer A Picture With Your Items In It*

Stage 5: *Label Your Items*

Stage 6: *Select An Item From Your Item List*

Stage 7: *Sell Your Items In Instagram Stories*

4. Powerhouse Promotion

Powerhouse promoting is another procedure you can use to sell your items on the web. This is the point at which a powerhouse works with your image to advance an item or administration you give in return for installment or free stuff.

This powerhouse, as an individual with believability in a specific specialty, will capitalize on their leverage over their devotees to advance your objective positively, prompting deals.

Powerhouse showcasing can be an incredible way for you to stretch out beyond your rivals and construct your image without making heaps of new satisfied or publicizing.

This promoting strategy is utilized broadly over Instagram, Snapchat, Facebook, and other web-based entertainment stages, yet should be possible really on any internet-based channel assuming that it's famous for your crowd.

THE MOST EFFECTIVE METHOD TO SELL ON THE WEB: HOT SELLING THOUGHTS STYLISH

Anything that you've found out about beginning an internet-based business, it's most likely obvious. A cutthroat jungle gym challenges even the savviest business people, yet the mind-boggling agreement is that you begin figuring out how to sell on the web...

Perhaps the most awesome aspect of it is that you can sell online past the lines of your city, your nation, or even landmass while never leaving your work area! When you get everything rolling, practically anybody from any place on the planet can turn into your client.

However, Where Do You Begin?

There are straightforward ways of sorting out some way to sell on the web, and they all come from the responses to three fundamental inquiries - why, what, and how?

Here is an aid of all that you want to be familiar with regarding how to sell on the web. It couldn't get any more straightforward.

Why Think About How to Sell Online Is Really Tactful?

Could you, at any time, forecast your existence without the internet? No information, no injury-time shopping, no feline recordings... Let's just stop there.

That is unequivocally why the Internet business industry is experiencing its brilliant age. Everybody is associated and nestled in their little web-based rises without any expectation of returning to the former ways. Connecting to this pattern is starting to seem to be the savviest method for beginning an internet-based business.

Here's more on why:

1. **<u>Your Business Follows Wherever You Go</u>**

We should move this one first — disregard *real* getaways without a PC, essentially for the primary year or somewhere in the vicinity.

At your discovery of how to sell stuff on the internet, any spot on the planet can become your office, and as a general rule, you'll wind up showing up on Saturday or Sunday, evenings, and occasions. The major contrast is that you'll do it cheerfully.

Work from the river side or your grandmother's garden — anywhere you go, you're simply a click (and a Wi-Fi connection) away from reaching your business. All that you in all actuality do should drive you towards progress.

2. **Destitute? Start a business with a small cost!**

The excellence of the web-based world is that you can get the business going with next to no underlying venture. It depends on the kind of business you're proposing to start, yet for this article, we're accepting you have your brain set on running a web-based store. Furthermore, regarding selling web-based, outsourcing is by all accounts the go-to procedure.

With the minimum overheads, for example, paying for the facilitating of your site and running a few internet advertisement, you can sell items on the internet and build a profitable business in only a few months.

Also, it's not a dream of some sort or another. There are real examples for winning adversity to illustrate it.

3. **You Can Bring In Cash Day In And Day Out**

While physical shops are restricted to opening and closing times, online stores run 24/7. Constantly.

It doesn't take a virtuoso to see the potential in this plan of action. If you have a consistent stream of traffic coming to your store and you upgrade your transformations to a decent norm, you can procure latently while you rest.

This addresses one more significant advantage of selling on the web - if done well, it tends to be a sweet wellspring of leftover pay. It is less time-escalated than, say, running a physical store since you needn't bother with it to be available consistently. With computerized stock administration and a hearty web-based promoting plan, you can dominate how to sell things online with very little contribution from your side.

4. **There's A Myriads Of Space To Build-up.**

Business visionaries frequently need to twist around in reverse to continue to build their deals. While you might have the most sizzling items in stock, they very well may be elusive new clients and keep them faithful to your business. Deciding to sell online can fix this issue in a jiffy.

As per the most recent Internet business stats, the number of web-based customers is rapidly developing and is expected to hit an incredible 2.14 billion in 2021.

The focal point? Business visionaries who are still going back and forth about web-based selling ought to make a move before they're left in the residue. Also, with such countless methodologies for selling on the web, it couldn't be easier to gain by the developing internet business pattern.

Presently, that sounds like a blessing from heaven.
Until you hit the following foundation of this cycle: What will I sell on the web?

WEB-BASED SELLING THOUGHTS: OBTAINING ITEMS WHEN YOU'RE STUCK

We should pass on the subject of how to sell online briefly and center around WHAT things to sell all things being equal. Finding a beneficial thought is not a simple errand. However, you'll be shocked at where you can track down item suggestions. In some cases, the response may be flying under the radar.

1. **Piggyback On Patterns**

Who would rather not be a pioneer? A spearheading virtuoso with a weighty thought? It's a bursting dream of numerous business visionaries. However, the

Internet business world isn't generally kind to remarkable web-based selling thoughts.

To get the deals motor running, a web-based store necessities to serve popularity in a market and source top items to sell in 2021.

At the point when you're on the chase after a lucrative thought, it pays off to stand by listening to what the clients need. Indeed, I'm discussing the top-rated records, pattern reports, and item curation records.

Begin your underlying item research by projecting a wide net. To begin with, survey the new and impending patterns on internet-based retail goliaths, like eBay, Amazon, or Etsy. What are the month's top picks, most loved items, or smash-hit things? Might you at any point detect a specific pattern like tones, shapes, textures, or examples?

At the point when you have a harsh thought of what you need to offer on the web, now is the ideal time to figure out how to source these items for your internet-based store. Furthermore, one of the most mind-blowing spots to search for outsourcing item thoughts is Oberlo.

Give Oberlo an intensive look, and you're nearly ensured to track down something that addresses your issues. For instance, items with over 500 orders in the beyond 30 days are probably going to sell well. Hop on these items rapidly, so you can stretch out beyond the opposition.

Your next legitimate step is to pick high-edge items.

2. Go For The Gold

What is important by the day's end is how much cash you get to keep. Solid edges will decide the future of your internet business, so you ought to give your best to put your time and exertion into items that will yield the best outcomes.

The typical online business gross edge is roughly 40%. Be that as it may, each market and each item are unique, so you ought to invest energy in dissecting the opposition and the going rate.

The absolute least demanding strategies you can use to amplify the benefits incorporate tracking down winning items to sell, putting them at the front of your promoting drives and strategically pitching efforts, and adding varieties of the top-rated things (think various varieties, sizes, and shapes).

Oberlo has a net revenue number cruncher that will provide you with a superior thought of your choices.

3. **Continue In The Strides Of Other Web-based Business Champs.**

Why attempt to rehash an already solved problem? Profiting by valuable assets, for example, Oberlo's 100+ Best Items to Sell in 2021 digital book and 'What to Sell' segment, is a definitive easy route to starting an effective web-based store. Cheer up from putting resources into a specific thought since another person is likewise making it happen - the internet-based world is large enough for all hawkers.

INSTRUCTIONS TO SELL ITEMS ONLINE EFFECTIVELY

Presently, we're prepared to address the subject of how to sell on the web. Since we discuss all things internet business here in Oberlo, we will examine how to sell items on the web. The following are a couple of procedures that you can set in motion easily.

1. **Utilize Existing Deals Entryways.**

You can sell online through commercial centers like Amazon, eBay, or Etsy. However, this methodology has its upsides and downsides.

On the genius side, there's a laid-out, huge local area of returning clients that you can get to. What's more, for somebody who's simply figuring out how to offer on the web, it's no joking matter to have the option to take advantage of a tremendous pool of online customers that as of now trust the stage.

Another huge addition to web-based business amateurs is the amazing chance to test their interest in the items they offer.

You could test one-item store thoughts in which you fabricate a brand around a solitary item.

When you lay out a fair of what's well known, now is the right time to begin constructing a web-based store. Assuming that you make one with Shopify, it's not difficult to associate famous deals channels to your store.

All in all, why shift the technique when it begins returning a benefit? Many reasons. To begin with, enormous commercial centers like Amazon, eBay, or Etsy will charge you a commission for each deal. Second, selling through an outsider will keep you from building an individual relationship with your clients.

Generally, you will not have the option to catch their email addresses, give valuable substance, or run your missions to produce more deals. Likewise, commercial centers can close your store whenever, which is an exorbitant and harmful cycle to go through.

2. Sell Through Web-based Entertainment Stages

Alongside commercial centers, web-based entertainment channels like Facebook and Instagram permit you to get your items before forthcoming clients. For example, you can set up a Facebook shop to exhibit your stock to Facebook clients. Those intrigued can then add your things to their truck and look at them on the stage straightforwardly. Be that as it may, if you'd prefer to make an autonomous Internet business site,

Facebook offers multiple ways of selling on the web; you can utilize your Facebook Business Page, run promotions, and sell items at Facebook gatherings.

Virtual entertainment permits you to work with powerhouses. You can offer examples of your things to powerhouses as a trade-off for hollers. Recognize some powerhouses in your specialty by looking for pertinent hashtags, then collaborate with them to advance your items through stories, recordings, and posts, and the sky is the limit from there.

3. **Make Your Outsourcing Site**

On account of stages like Shopify, setting up your site is simpler than at any time in recent memory. You can exploit free preliminaries and unending web-based assets to get it going in only a couple of days.

Likewise, you can introduce an outsourcing application to dispose of the problem of purchasing and putting away stock. It's an extraordinary method for offering on the web because of its many benefits. However, the most significant is, obviously, the least arrangement costs - since you don't have to purchase the stock or deal with a distribution center.

There's likewise the capacity to offer a broad choice of items, which assists with scaling rapidly, and the unimaginable adaptability that accompanies the way that you can maintain your business from any place on the planet. The ideal combo of potential and opportunity is drawing in computerized travelers and hawkers.

In any case, it's not bother-free. With so many examples of overcoming adversity powering the premium in this market, the opposition to selling online is high and developing, so it's pivotal you get your work done before committing.

A portion of the other most normally referred to issues, like tracking down the right providers, can be tackled by incorporating existing web-based business devices. With 2,000-in addition to five-star surveys and a free Pioneer plan,

Oberlo is one of the most famous decisions with regard to bringing in items to your web-based store and overseeing stock.

We should take a gander at it along these lines - a web-based store is practically allowed to be set up. No underlying venture implies there are not many dangers implied, and the variables deciding your business' prosperity are completely in your control. On the off chance that you have the opportunity and assets for grinding away alone, recollect - sooner is better compared to later.

24 METHODS FOR MAKING YOUR MOST MEMORABLE INTERNET BUSINESS DEAL (WITHOUT SPENDING A TON)

As a web-based shipper, it is however emblematic, as it seems to be important to make your most memorable deal.

Finishing the major deal sounds sufficiently clear, yet the hopefulness and consolation it brings can make it the greatest defining moment in the existence of your business.

In any case, don't let the basic idea of a first deal deceives you. Getting that first client can here and there be a long, strenuous fight.

To make the fight simpler to win, underneath are 24 certain-fire ways of making your most memorable online business deal without spending a ton.

1. **Send Free Samples Of Forces To Be Reckoned With**

The web is loaded with interesting bloggers, writers, business visionaries, and vloggers from many enterprises and specialties. You simply have to track down the right ones.

A considerable lot of them have enormous followings via virtual entertainment and steadfast crowds on their sites.

Sending a free example of your item to powerhouses inside your industry or connected with it here and there offers you a chance to tell them you value their work with a little gift. Ideally, you will get a notice on one of their locales or stages.

This can bring about a spike in rush hour gridlock and online entertainment supporters, however, you'll likewise have an endorsement from industry specialists.

A helpful asset for powerhouses is Neil Patel's conclusive manual for force to be reckoned with focusing on, which lets you know all that you want to be aware of to get your image under pertinent, significant noses.

2. **Begin Writing For A Blog**

If you're not previously running a blog related to your store or item, then you're passing up the boundless capability of content showcasing.

By delivering free, important substance, you make trust in your image and keep individuals informed. Contributing to a blog likewise gives you content to share via online entertainment and assists you with the positioning of web search tools.

To begin, consider all the beginning-stage inquiries individuals have about your items and industry. Utilize your blog to respond to these inquiries as individual articles.

For instance, guests to the Shopify blog may be keen on finding out about web-based business and outsourcing. Thus, they made content that positions for terms like "how to sell on the web" and "how to outsource."

Also, you can utilize your blog to offer tips, instructional exercises, and assets connected with your items and the way of life around your items.

If you can make epic substance consistently, you'll start to see the force of content showcasing utilizing web-based entertainment shares, web crawlers, etc. This is all canvassed in our manual for content promotion.

3. **Construct An Email Rundown**

Developing an email list is significant to make your most memorable deal — and it doesn't need to cost you a thing.

As indicated by DMA, email has a typical return for money invested of $42 per $1 spent — not excessively pitiful. Building your email list, notwithstanding, costs very little.

Having a rundown of messages from past and potential clients implies you can get your data, items, and content into their letter boxes. Conversely, refreshes made to your Facebook page and Twitter handle won't ever arrive at your whole following, because of time region contrasts and web-based entertainment calculations.

Begin fabricating your email list by including an email membership structure on your site.

Here is a sharp method for persuading guests to pursue your rundown. Rather than essentially saying "Join our Bulletin," offer an impetus or some sort of significant worth for joining. Thin Teatox offers the opportunity to win a free item consistently, so they exhibit that proposal to urge individuals to join.

If you want some more counsel on the most proficient method to get everything rolling, here's an ideal novice's manual for email promoting.

4. **Support A (Face To Face Or Virtual) Occasion**

Supporting an occasion can make all the difference — on the off chance that you utilize the right methodology.

To start with, guarantee you select the right occasion to support. Look for occasions where participants are probably going to be keen on your item, and afterward, figure out the number of customers that will be in participation. Then begin arranging them by cost.

Don't send a company of promoters to set up a table and hand-out flyers. Assuming that potential clients are joining in, you'll be more imaginative to fabricate connections.

Display a portion of your most interesting items to recount your story, get people talking, and give immediate compensates like coupons and free stickers as a trade-off for email list memberships and web-based entertainment follows.

5. Interview Industry Forces To Be Reckoned With

Recall the significance of the content showcasing I referenced before. All things being equal, contacting an industry force to be reckoned with is an amazing method for creating an epic substance.

Interviews work since they are shared benefit circumstances. The interviewee becomes more open, while the questioner gets their hands on some hot item for their distribution, which, in this case, is your blog.

Capitalize on the meeting by posing pertinent inquiries about their lives and professions, yet in addition to the business in general. This will guarantee fanatics of the force to be reckoned with experiencing their character, while others will esteem their master's guidance.

6. Pull A PR Trick

Assuming that you need that first deal quickly, pulling a PR trick could get the job done.

Similar to viral recordings, a PR stunt can move your image into distinction. Assuming that executed well, you'll trade customary tedious brand promoting with moment exposure, acquiring your steadfast devotees and clients all the while.

A PR stunt comprises accomplishing something uncommon, unbelievable, diverting, or sufficiently noteworthy to deserve media consideration.

Thus, your store could profit from lots of connections from power news sources, which is perfect for both traffic temporarily and Website design enhancement in the long haul.

No organization pulls a preferred PR stunt over Virgin. Their pioneer, Richard Branson, has spruced up as a wedding lady of the hour, leaped off a club rooftop, acted like a Zulu fighter, driven a tank down Fifth Road in New York City, and flown an inflatable all over the planet, among numerous other newsworthy things.

To get your imaginative energies pumping, investigate Business visionary's rundown of the top 19 effective showcasing stunts. They've covered everything from silly tattoos to left-gave burgers. Keep in mind, a decent PR stunt doesn't need lots of money or a major brand to pull it off. It simply requires innovativeness.

7. **Try Different Things With Google Advertisements**

Google Promotions (previously AdWords) is Google's massively well-known pay-per-click publicizing network that permits online retailers to put ads on virtually every Google query items page, YouTube video, and accomplice site.

Who would have zero desire to rank in the main three of a pursuit question that drives deals? This shows up when you type "Samsung television" into Google. Note that the primary outcomes are paid promotions from Samsung.

The excellence of Google Promotions lies in its speed and monstrous reach. In only a couple of moments, you can set up and send off a promoting effort that gets your message, picture, or even video promotions seen by programs all around the web.

Utilizing the AdWords lobby choices, you can make designated advertisements that are set off and shown close by Google look when Web programs look for predefined watchwords. Furthermore, your advertisements likewise will show up on sites and articles which contain comparative watchwords.

8. **Share The Heap With Partner Advertising**

Trying to sell your items alone can be a troublesome task, so why not share the stuff with others?

Member showcasing is the point at which you let others market your items and send you site traffic. Consequently, you pay them a level of any deals that starts from their endeavors. Track their promoting endeavors can by giving an exceptional hyperlink or coupon code.

For instance, a site proprietor might post your offshoot interface for a blue sweater available to be purchased on your site. On the off chance that one of his site guests taps the connection and purchases the blue sweater, you'll have made a transaction, and as a member, the site manager will be qualified for a part of that deal. The incredible thing about this selling system is that you possibly pay if you make a deal.

The progress of associate promoting relies vigorously upon the kinds of items you sell and the commission rate you reward subsidiary accomplices.

9. **Offer Discounts To Different Retailers**

Offering to customers is fine, however, selling discounts may be exactly what you want to get the deals moving.

One of the principal benefits of selling discounts is the undeniable expansion in income. There may be a smaller overall revenue, yet the amount can compensate for the difference.

Also, you're empowering different organizations and affiliates to advertise for you, getting the message out about your product as they get it themselves. This implies selling discounts could in a roundabout way support your shopper deals.

For a compressed lesson on the rudiments of offering a discount, look at a Business person's manual for beginning a discount dispersion business.

10. **Distribute An Official Statement**

Tons of new web-based stores push out public statements to draw in media consideration, however, fizzle.

It is a less valuable methodology than it used to be, however it can in any case work. Getting disregarded by each media source while disseminating another public statement is debilitating and is frequently a tremendous misuse of assets.

The Key To Getting Seen Is Basic. Try Not To Distribute A Junky Public Statement!!!

Ensure your news, most importantly, really is newsworthy. Try not to expect a gigantic reaction except if you're giving the public something genuinely fascinating to find out about. Likewise, a public statement ought to be introduced in a manner that is succinct and proficient, without being excessively dreary.

Copyblogger has sorted out six methods for composing an incredible public statement, making sense of all that from staying away from language to making an attractive title.

11. **Focus On Location Examination**

The way of behaving of every site guest from the section to leave assists you with understanding the reason why you are selling, and all the more significantly, why you're not.

Your site details (or investigation) will show you what your clients are doing on your webpage, including which website pages they enter, the time they spend on specific pages, and the course they take to leave your webpage. At times, a few instruments will show extra data, for example, the way often a client visits your site.

It won't cost you a penny, by the same token. Google Examination is free help, permitting you to quantify your traffic in additional ways than you can imagine.

Here is a model from Marvel Berry. You can see consistent traffic up until early January when there is an enormous leap. They took a gander at their information and saw that the leap came from StumbleUpon, which could be a decent pointer that the social channel merits going after further, either naturally or utilizing a paid position.

While you're battling for your most memorable deal, it's critical to invest energy in dissecting your traffic in Google Examination.

No one can tell what you will realize.

If you want a hand beginning, Essentially Business offers an extensive Google Examination guide, covering all that you want to be aware of.

12. **Run An Overview**

Purchaser reviews are an optimal instrument for getting legitimate input. Not at all like your loved ones, shoppers have no doubts about making you feel horrible by picking at your website architecture or your showcasing material.

To run your special review, you can utilize online applications like Study Monkey and Qualaroo to make online overviews.

QuestionPro has a rundown of 45+ inquiries to pose to internet business guests, which can assist you with capitalizing on your criticism.

13. **Network Via Virtual Entertainment Gatherings Or Discussions**

Online conversation discussions and web-based entertainment bunches are incredible spots to share industry tips and counsel, answer questions, and gain a client or two.

Use Google or Facebook to find dynamic discussions and gatherings that straightforwardly connect with your specialty. Twitter talks and conflict can likewise be home to specialty conversation gatherings. At the point when you post, guarantee you're not disrupting any guidelines when you advance your image or items. Get to know the cutoff points and limitations of the gathering, and stick to them. Utilizing your gathering symbol, mark, and profile page to advance your image is normally well inside the guidelines.

No gathering will endure consistent advancement, or presents loaded with joins on your site. Moreover, it makes you look malicious. In this way, save it basically by posting barely enough for individuals to see your movement, however insufficient to comprise spam.

Two well-known business-centered gatherings worth getting dynamic on are Computerized Point and Champion Discussion, the two of which have flourishing, supportive networks.

14. Construct The Right Connections

It's not what you know, it's whom you know. Building the right connections, both on the web and disconnected, can go about as your entry progresses.

Regardless of what kind of item you sell or which industry you work in, there are similar organizations out there, and you want to become a close acquaintance with them.

Try to fabricate associations with others that are firmly adjusted to your business but not immediate contenders.

For instance, providers, web journals, and sites that emphasize your industry would be great, as they can assist with giving you buyer input and proposition special arrangements without stepping on your computerized toes.

Take online business Gathering, for instance. Working through a Facebook bunch, they have north of 2,500 individuals sharing guidance, giving criticism, and giving some assistance whenever the situation allows.

15. Offer A Challenge Or Giveaway

Everyone cherishes free stuff, and assuming that you're hoping to develop some trust while sending off your deals endeavors, a challenge or giveaway could assist you with doing exactly that.

Not exclusively can challenges and giveaways assist you to construct significant inbound connections, but they likewise are an extraordinary method for showing potential clients that you can be relied upon and that your image implies business.

It's memorabilia's essential you don't need to begin hugely. Bother Tea ran a straightforward challenge on their Facebook page.
This challenge costs no cash to run and reasonably required a couple of moments to assemble.

Online administrations like ViralSweep and Glimmer permit you to run such challenges and giveaways web-based, assisting you with keeping things straightforward and proficient without all the additional work.

16. **Start Tweeting On Twitter**

Twitter's straightforwardness makes it one of the best ways of drawing in with your objective market. A phenomenal technique for finding potential clients is to proactively look for individuals' tweeting inquiries concerning your industry and contact them in a supportive manner.

The thought isn't to pitch or try to notice your items - simply be useful. For instance, when Gary Vaynerchuk was running Wine Library, he would look at "Chardonnay" on Twitter and find individuals posing related inquiries.
All he did was offer counsel; he won't ever pitch.
Subsequently, individuals would normally look further into what his identity was, and eventually find his business.

This is only one of many Twitter procedures that can make all the difference for your marketing projections.

If you want some genuine instances of how to nail Twitter showcasing, investigate the Twitter profile of online gems store Lola Rose, which could show you some things.

17. **Make Associations On LinkedIn**

LinkedIn is the workplace block of the Web. You'll track down experts and chiefs, everything being equal, flaunting their capacities and associating with others.

After you set up your online business profile, you can start doing likewise for yourself. You may not make any immediate deals through LinkedIn, however, you'll find a variety of chances with different organizations, providers, and related sites.

LinkedIn Gatherings likewise are a heavenly method for drawing in other entrepreneurs in your industry. There are lots of public and confidential gatherings set up for explicit specialties, permitting you to post questions and speak with different individuals.

To discover a few significant Gatherings, search on LinkedIn or ask your supporters what bunches they suggest.

18. Go Visual With Pinterest, Instagram, Or TikTok

Pinterest, Instagram, and most, as of late TikTok, permit you to adopt a somewhat unique strategy to draw in customers.

These stages are the ideal spot to introduce the innovativeness and enthusiasm that goes into your business in the background. Snap photos of your items, take recordings of the assembling system and recount a story with pictures. Continuously hold back nothing conceivable. Individuals love excellence.

Need some visual motivation? Dissolve Beauty care products began as another brand however presently has over 2.7 million devotees on Instagram. They are working effectively on Instagram promoting, developing a brand picture and a following with their wonderful photos.

19. Remember Facebook

Beyond a shadow of a doubt, Facebook is a web-based entertainment force to be reckoned with.

Influence your own Facebook profile and your business page to draw in companions, family, and colleagues and get individuals to discuss your items.

Get imaginative with announcements and interface on open gatherings and fan pages applicable to your specialty.

Remembering Facebook Promotions is likewise significant. Similar to Google Advertisements, you can make designated missions to draw in preferences, make deals, and advance your image.

A famous blow-drying salon in Toronto called Drybar has a very connected Facebook people group of lots of 80,000 who talk about everything blow-drying.

20. **Take Down The Opposition On The Correlation Between Shopping Motors**

Most customers like to look around before making a buy, and that incorporates a visit to web search tools and locales like Amazon.

Famous motors incorporate Google Shopping, PriceGrabber, Amazon, and a scope of others, all contrasting numerous items and stores at the same time.

Here is a model from The Find where I'm looking at a cost examination on my #1 hot sauce.

To get seen, you want to carry on reasonably every motor, remain serious concerning cost, and play the cat-and-mouse game while you try to figure out which motor suits you the best and gives you the best return for the money invested.

21. **Make An Infographic**

An infographic is a precisely exact thing the name suggests, a chart of data — and they are truly simple to make nowadays utilizing instruments like Canva.

Infographics are gold concerning social offers and web crawler traffic. As per Content Advertising Establishment, 65% of advertisers use infographics for content showcasing — and they can without much of a stretch twofold your traffic.

As indicated by UnBounce, which has made a rousing and Nitty gritty manual for promoting infographics, individuals who are looking for infographics like you might have a hard time believing. They can likewise assist with drawing in joins, which is great for website design enhancement.

22. **Plan Your Store To Look Like It**

Initial feelings mean the world, and concerning selling on the web, initial feelings depend vigorously on website architecture.

Guests should have the option to comprehend your image and items without a lot of looking over or investigating. Moreover, exploring your inventory ought to be simple, if not charming.

Also, making your store receptive to cell phones is urgent. The greater part of all web traffic occurs on a cell phone, so ensure your webpage works and looks great on telephones and tablets.

Assuming you are utilizing WordPress search for subjects that are explicitly intended for online business.

23. **Have A Spring Store**

Since your store started online doesn't mean it needs to remain on the web. A web-based business spring-up store could be exactly what you want to supplement your internet-based presence.

Not at all, like customary blocks and-mortar premises, a spring-up store is brief and costs substantially less.

A spring-up store is about the area. You can open a spring-up store at ranchers' markets, workmanship fairs, shopping centers, exhibitions, and some other spots individuals accumulate. Simply ensure you're set up in a space that is noticeable and where your objective market will meander.

A spring-up store likewise can go about as an incredibly disconnected showcasing station. You can utilize your store to pass out coupons to be utilized in your web-based store, and you can gather email addresses and online entertainment adherents.

For certain thoughts on the best way to get your spring-up store moving, the Web-based Entertainment Inspector incorporated 51 spring-up store thoughts to rouse you.

24. Archive Your Send Off On Reddit

Reddit is a socially controlled information and diversion site where clients submit content. All the more critically, Reddit is where you can draw in countless committed adherents and clients.

Utilizing the r/business visionary subreddit specifically, you can present your image, gain input from customers, and learn examples, while likewise advancing your items.

However, the interaction must be one of compromise. Walk those pioneering redditors through your excursion, take them in the background, detail your missteps, and uncover a character to acquire clients, yet fans, as well.

A splendid instance of utilizing Reddit to advance an internet-based store is what the folks at Beardbrand did. The facial hair-preparing experts archived their send-off on the r/business visionary subreddit, getting important counsel from endorsers and clients while rewarding them through customary updates and inside data.

Here is the organizer presenting a report on the r/business person's local area.

Note the number of up-votes and remarks this post got. Reddit can be a very useful asset, however, it can likewise be whimsical. Carve out an opportunity to get to comprehend the local area before making a plunge.

Setting up your web-based business store is no simple undertaking, however, there are a lot of web-based customers prepared to spend cash on the web.

The 24 systems recorded above are heavenly ways of kicking start deals for your internet-based store.

With the right methodology, you will require just a small bunch of the systems recorded above to make the first of numerous deals. If you want a little assistance getting traffic, connect.

Which technique will you use to make your most memorable web-based business deal?

DEVELOP YOUR TRAFFIC

THE FORCE OF FAME

Does Fame Liken To More Business? Do Well-known Organizations Get More Business?

In school, the well-known kids generally appeared to be the best. They were many times savvy, interesting and appealing. Perhaps they were remarkable competitors. Perhaps they likewise got passing marks. Everybody loved and begrudged them, including instructors.

Does likewise turn out as expected for organizations? Consider famous organizations, like Amazon, Apple, Tesla, Google, Microsoft, even Facebook, and Twitter. Every single one of these organizations is (or at times, was) driven by a charming pioneer. Subsequently, you'd expect that famous organizations truly do get more business.

There's More Going On Behind The Scenes.

Fame in business today is estimated in likes, notices, devotees, and snaps. These are among the numerous measurements followed and logged via the website, streamlining trained professionals. Promoted as showing market infiltration, age, orientation, area, and orders each like notice, adherent, and snap even pay level. Large information is the means through which organizations measure their ubiquity.

In this sort of prominence challenge, the objective isn't really to get more business, yet to surpass your rivals' numbers. It's as of now not a necessary evil, yet a finish to itself. Assuming being well known was a definitive objective in business, you'd see fewer bookkeepers and more advertisers. There could be increasingly big limits to charming fans — because the group with the most fans wins, correct?

Contrasting Organizations With Sports Groups
1. Here and there, organizations and sports groups are comparable:
2. Both put a gigantic exertion into marking and name acknowledgment.
3. Both effectively participate in winning and keeping fans.
4. If effective, both partake in a strong groundwork of stalwart devotees.
5. Sports groups, similar to organizations, need positive media inclusion.
6. Sports groups have a dedicated nearby following, like effective physical organizations.

The most famous groups, similar to organizations, are viewed as champs practically regardless of what they do, except if and until they make a shocking advertising blunder.

Yet, in other significant ways, the two contrast fiercely. For instance:

Sports groups can encounter a terrible year — or even an awful 10 years — yet be a practical venture; organizations can support a specific number of yearly misfortunes before they need to tap out.

Avid supporters go to games, regardless of whether it's pulling for the opposition.

Sports groups, not at all like organizations, need wins on the field to give their fans something to cheer about.

A title prize can support fans for 10 years; businesses should continually adjust and develop — their fans all the more normally inquire, "How have you helped me recently?"

Although they are organizations, sports establishments don't gauge progress in dollars. Any remaining organizations don't gauge progress in wins.

The Worth Of Fame

Organizations burn through hundreds to thousands of dollars consistently via online entertainment. Some post every day or even hourly. And afterward, there's the obligation to answer remarks. It requires investment and cash to deal with a functioning online entertainment account. Presently duplicate that by 10, to incorporate every one of the different virtual entertainment stages, and you find out about the genuine expense.

However, what's the genuine worth of those preferences, notices, supporters, and snaps? Do they channel genuine individuals toward deals? The response is complicated, however; it depends less on preferences and supporters and more on on-site traffic.

Does Fame Get More Business For Organizations?

Online entertainment creates brand mindfulness, no question, as it gets a business' name before many individuals, on the off chance that they're fruitful. Web-based entertainment is likewise an incredible spot to deal with a business' client experience. In the exceptionally open foundation of online entertainment, your business can alleviate objections and encourage diplomats. These are positive things.

However, most internet business happens on an organization's site. So site traffic and online deals recount the story. To get more business, an organization needs to ask virtual entertainment devotees and fans to visit their site. Without that association, being well known is not any more pertinent than being named Imprint.

Steering the Results

The last piece of the situation to get more business is adjusting the expense of all online entertainment commitment to real deals from all that movement. It's perfect if your organization can produce $10,000 in gross income from web-based entertainment contacts. In any case, it's significantly less thrilling on the off chance that you're paying $8,000 per month to keep up with that site presence. It's as yet a success regarding hard numbers, yet the proportion isn't promising.

It depends on where you are in the cycle. On the off chance that you're simply beginning your web-based entertainment crusade, you might have no place to go except for up. In any case, assuming you've been busy for a year, that $10,000 in income might address the high-water mark. There are elements to investigate, for example, diminishing the expenses while keeping up with the income stream. Just you, as the entrepreneur, can decide whether it merits going on for this situation.

Fame, as a rule, doesn't get more business for your organization. It is just an indication of brand mindfulness and brand acknowledgment. Both of those are up-sides, however, they don't necessarily convert into additional benefits. Be careful with the virtual entertainment game.

THE STRENGTH OF WEB-BASED COMMERCIAL CENTERS IN THE RETAIL BUSINESS

Taking into account the development of online commercial centers, many hopeful business visionaries are currently hoping to send off their internet business commercial centers

Assessments communicated by businessperson givers are their own.

You're perusing businessperson India, a worldwide establishment of businessperson Media.

As per details, 33% of purchasers start their web-based venture from online commercial centers like Amazon, eBay, Flipkart, and so on.

Moreover, deals on web-based commercial centers represented 52% of worldwide web-based retail deals. Clients like to sell their items at online commercial centers. The big number of providers or dealers at Amazon, Uber, Airbnb, and so on is the best proof. Inarguably, this is the time of online commercial centers.

1. Why Online Commercial Centers Are Overall #1?

There is a mutually beneficial arrangement for everybody in internet-based commercial centers. The commercial center proprietor can acquire a great measure of commission from the merchants and promoters, clients can partake in the better nature of administration and serious evaluation, and dealers can sell their items without site arrangement and overseeing cost.

Not just commercial centers like Amazon, eBay, and Alibaba are assuming control over the world, however the web-based commercial centers like Mudah (Malaysia-based commercial center), Merry go round (Singapore-based commercial center) and Rakuten (Japan-based commercial center) that serve the neighborhood locales have additionally developed incredibly throughout the long term.

Taking into account the development of online commercial centers, many hopeful business people are presently hoping to send off their own web-based business commercial centers.

2. What Sort Of Web-based Commercial Center Could You Have At Any Point Assemble?

Here are various types of online commercial centers that you can send off:

- ➢ *Online Interview Commercial Center:* Utilizing this kind of commercial center, individuals can interface with experts like specialists, legal counselors, and specialists to get exhortations or administrations.

- ➢ *Online Administrations Commercial Center:* This sort of commercial center permits individuals to straightforwardly profit administrations, for example, online visits and bundles, inn booking, and membership administrations from vendors. Make my outing and Airbnb the best instances of an internet-based administration commercial center.

- ➢ *Online Items Conveyance Commercial Center:* In this kind of commercial center, individuals can look at and purchase items from various merchants. Then, at that point, the commercial center administrator conveys the items to them for the vendors' benefit. Amazon, Flipkart, and Zomato are the best models in this class.

- ➢ *B2B Commercial Center:* Increasingly more B2B purchasers are going to the web for examination and buying on the web. In a B2B commercial center, merchants can offer their items at a discount rate to different organizations. Alibaba and Walmart are two well-known B2B commercial centers.

> **C2C Commercial Center:** In a C2C commercial center, clients can sell straightforwardly to different clients. OLX and Taobao are famous C2C commercial centers.

> **Rental Commercial Center:** You can begin a rental commercial center like Uber, and so on to be essential for the developing sharing economy.

Must-have Elements In A Web-based Commercial Center

Various sorts of web-based commercial centers might have various types of elements. Notwithstanding, there are sure highlights that are expected in each commercial center, including:

1. Separate Merchant Dashboard
2. Different Regulatory Access
3. Item Index Framework
4. Different Installment Entryways
5. The Smoothed-out Merchant Payout Framework
6. Item Appraising And Survey Framework
7. Appraisals And Surveys For Vendors
8. High-level Ordesellersement Framework
9. Responsive Site
10. Website Optimization Agreeable Framework
11. Portable Applications For Clients, Administrators, And Vendors
12. Mechanized Task Handling

13. Detailing And Information Investigation For Administrators And Vendors
14. Incorporation With Outsider Instruments And POS Frameworks
15. Enlistment Pages For Clients And Merchants
16. Transporting Techniques
17. Area-based Search
18. Mass Import From Various Stages Like Amazon, Ebay, And So On.
19. Demand For Citation Includes (B2B)

The Component Rundown Can Be Reached According To A Business Necessities.

4 MOTIVATIONS BEHIND WHY A WEB-BASED BUSINESS IS THE BEST SPECULATION YOU WILL AT ANY POINT MAKE

Business visionaries are an uncommon variety of people who are continually investigating new business open doors.

Some search out new open doors all alone while others are continually being tried out by groundbreaking thoughts.

Most chances, regardless of how great they could sound, turn out to be a finished cash-sucking bad dream because of costly above, slow versatility, and low edges. Online organizations, in any case, can be extremely engaging because they don't have the conventional obstacles that most new pursuits face. Coming up next are four justifications for why online organizations are the best speculation business visionaries can make.

1. Offers Staggering Adaptability

Few out of every odd single internet-based business will naturally transform into a gigantic accomplishment with fast dramatic development. Numerous business people start a web-based business thinking clients are naturally going to find them and deals will pour in because they have a brief impression on the Web. They imagine that a couple of tweets and some Facebook posts are all it will require accelerating an internet-based business into a virtual ATM.

Scaling any business is difficult, whether it is a physical area or a web-based business. However, an internet-based business enjoys benefits. For example, a physical retail location has a characterized crowd, ordinarily a span from the business area. This doesn't confine an internet-based business and can market to an overall crowd.

When an effective promoting and publicizing technique is distinguished, an internet-based business can open up its objective and increment financial plan to develop exceptionally quickly.

2. Gives Boundless Opportunity

Numerous business people are attracted to online organizations due to the opportunity they offer. Current innovation, PCs, tablets, business applications, and VOIP correspondence frameworks are only a portion of the devices that permit organizations to be worked in any area. Whenever you are in a Starbucks investigation — I ensure somebody is dealing with their web-based business or startup while associated with Wi-Fi and tasting their #1 espresso.

Not Being Attached To A Specific Area Or Work Area All Day Can Very Enable. A Few Business Visionaries Don't Have The Foggiest Idea Of How To Adjust The Opportunity And Crash And Burn With A Vengeance, While

Others Utilize The Opportunity As Inspiration To Work Much Harder. Try Not To Confuse The Opportunity With Time To Relax. Genuine Business Visionaries Regard The Opportunity And Comprehend That The Difficult Work Is Definitely Worth The Capacity To Invest More Energy With Their Families And Participate In Exercises That Most Pass Up Because They Are Essential For The All-day Grind.

3. **Low Above And High Edges**

An internet-based business will frequently permit you to dispose of a portion of the colossal expenses related to a disconnected business. In addition to the fact that you kill can things, for example, expensive office or retail space and long haul rent responsibilities, you can likewise take out tying up your cash in loading stock.

An outsourcing concurrence with the maker or a production-to-arrange plan can significantly diminish your monetary gamble and will permit you to keep up with additional reliable edges at a less forthright expense.

Assuming you had a business that sold caps and you brought five varieties: red, blue, green, yellow, and orange. In an actual physical area, you would have to keep each of the varieties in stock since you don't have the foggiest idea what cap individuals strolling through your entryway are coming to purchase.

If the yellow caps don't sell, you are compelled to limit them and assume a misfortune. Selling similar caps through outsourcing would mean you won't be left holding an unsold product that you have previously paid for.

4. **Acknowledgement For An Overall Market**

The delightful thing about a web-based business is the capacity to run it all day, every day without limits.

There are no topographical limits and there are no particular active times - - a web-based business can create income nonstop, even while you rest.

With a thoroughly examined web-based entertainment plan, site improvement, and paid media methodologies, an internet-based business can flourish.

You approach the globe right readily available. The advantage of having the option to target explicit states, districts, and nations give a high ground to online-based organizations.

Have you recently put resources into a web-based business or would you say you are thinking about it later on?

RUNDOWN

During youth and youthful adulthood, three main considerations can shape the arrangement of somebody's monetary outline. The first relies upon what a youngster catches wind of cash. On the off chance that a regarded grown-up shows a little child that cash is the foundation of all detestable, for instance, she probably will not foster a mentality that drives her to collect riches. The subsequent variable is how a youngster sees grown-ups collaborate with cash.

A child who watches his dad set aside cash by playing out his home fixes might decide to master cash-saving abilities as he grows up. The third element is the point at which a strangely sure or negative experience is conflated with cash, subsequently shading a kid's future monetary connections.

Assuming that a young lady's folks get into a fender bender while squabbling over cash, for instance, that young lady will probably experience difficulty examining funds with her accomplice when she becomes old. These variables can prompt hurtful and well-established monetary convictions, yet over the long haul, anybody can forget the perspectives that prompted their present monetary plan.

Until their monetary outline is analyzed and changed, individuals will always be unable to expand their pay or become their total assets. Indeed, even an aggressive laborer who decides to concentrate on methodologies like financial planning or business will not have the option to hold abundance without changing essential perspectives toward cash.

Monetary plans make sense of why many challenge victors rapidly lose their award cash, and why effective entrepreneurs can lose their underlying fortunes before collecting that abundance again in another undertaking. Assumptions so significantly impact considerations, sentiments, and results that individuals should change their viewpoint before they can economically gather more cash.

The people who need to change their monetary diagram can start by concentrating on the standards normal to the well-off. In the wake of concentrating on rich individuals' considerations and convictions, hopeful tycoons ought to create certifying, definitive explanations that they say without holding back consistently. By truly rehashing these statements and effectively attempting to phase out terrible vices, individuals can work on their monetary future and accomplish financial autonomy.

MONETARY PRESSURE FRUSTRATES INDIVIDUAL AND EXPERT DEVELOPMENT:

Although cash is much of the time considered the basis of all malevolence, it can be the answer for large numbers of life's difficulties. When morally procured, abundance can be utilized to determine or keep away from normal stressors like late bills or the absence of retirement reserve funds. Success can likewise give an inward feeling of harmony during transitory mishaps, similar to employment misfortune or unexpected ailment. Monetary flimsiness, then again, increments stress, diminishes certainty, and makes it harder to go ahead with carefully thought-out plans of action.

The pressure brought about by monetary unsteadiness doesn't just influence mental prosperity; it can likewise modify actual well-being. At the point when a stressor is connected with an impending risk, the body discharges chemicals that further develop usefulness in a survival circumstance.

Be that as it may, when a stressor is connected with existential danger, similar to an absence of assets, it delivers similar pressure chemicals at a steady rate. If feelings of anxiety stay high for a considerable length of time, the total effects of ongoing pressure can build the gamble of difficult sicknesses, similar to type 2 diabetes, heart failure, and stomach ulcers.

These dangers will generally compound since cash issues are frequently persistent.

Neglecting to address monetary insecurity, or essentially disregarding it, just increments combined pressure and makes the method involved with finding an answer seriously scary.

Figuring out how to oversee cash isn't just fundamental for enterprising undertakings; it is likewise a fundamental stage toward having a better existence.

You Can Launch Out Your Web-based Business NOW!

SHALOM!

www.ingramcontent.com/pod-product-compliance
Lightning Source LLC
Chambersburg PA
CBHW071125240526
45465CB00024B/1171